# On Chanting, Presence and Releasing

(Audio version available on:
http://bhaktishastra.com/on-chanting-presence-and-releasing/)

Satyadeva Das

Become Shakespeare.com

**First Published in 2022**

**Becomeshakespeare.com**

One Point Six Technologies Pvt Ltd
123, Building J2, Shram Seva Premises,
Wadala Truck Depot,
Wadala (East), Mumbai 400037, India
T: +91 8080226699



**ISBN** - 978-93-5458-880-8

# About the author:

Born in 1950, Satyadeva Das grew up in the San Francisco Bay Area. When he was 13 years old, he started to think about the true meaning of life. At the age of 19, he came to Tokyo – an event that he terms a fortunate accident. That is when he met his spiritual master, His Divine Grace A.C. Bhaktivedanta Swami Srila Prabhupada, the founder of the "International Society for Krishna Consciousness". This was beginning of his journey towards transcendental knowledge. Satyadeva Das got initiated the very same year by Srila

Prabhupada and for 51 years since then, he continues to be on the journey towards self-realization.

Satyadeva Das has been conducting workshops on awakening and yoga philosophy at yoga centres in California, Hawaii, China and Japan. He inspires people to live happily in the present, and understand the meaning of life. He distributes timeless wisdom found in ancient Indian spiritual philosophy. This book is based on transcripts of one of his two-day sessions with his students on this topic of attentive chanting.

Professionally, being a paramedic, he worked in intense stressful 911 emergency rescue teams for 25 years in the busy urban environments of Oakland and San Francisco, California. While rescuing injured people in disastrous conditions, he witnessed and dealt with death and traumatic situations on almost daily basis. It was very painful for him to make written reports of the details of each patient's conditions of suffering, since it reinforced the memories of their traumas. This led him to depression, to the point of being suicidal. This psychological "crisis" motivated him to go deeper into the India's 5000-years old wisdom. Satyadeva Das began to understand his own mind and consciousness. He practices using the present consciousness to overcome the repeated mental and behaviour patterns. This helps to release our anxiety, confusion and come back to the true self to help achieve a peaceful and happy life.

# Preface:

This book is especially aimed at practitioners of Bhakti yoga who perform "Japa" mantra meditation on the holy names of God, but for one reason or another have not experienced the inner transformation they were expecting. The admission that "I am not happy when chanting", or even worse, "chanting is a drudgery I have to do", can be a painfully shocking thing to admit to oneself and others. It takes honesty and courage to acknowledge that you have not yet realized the truth about yourself and continue to feel dissatisfied and unhappy with your life of chanting. If you find yourself described here in these words, then this book is for you. If you are someone who likes to absorb thoughts in an auditory manner, you may also listen to these lectures on the following link: http://bhaktishastra.com/on-chanting-presence-and-releasing/

I struggled for many years to chant and be happy. As a result of my own struggles to chant with attention and experience inner transformation, I am passionate about assisting Bhakti yogis who are not feeling happy with the quality of their spiritual practice, even after decades of sincere endeavour. The teaching on Presence and Releasing offered in this book is applicable to all forms of meditation, including mantra, and can powerfully aid those who want to deepen their practice to the point of chanting effortlessly.

In my experience, sometimes newcomers are not taught sufficiently the spiritual basics of attentive chanting and this lack of guidance may lead to less-than-optimal results for the chanter. Most beginner meditators are instructed to chant with reverence and attention and listen to the spiritual sound vibration of the holy names. Unfortunately, however, the beginner chanter may have not received clear and practical guidance about the process of chanting with consistent presence of awareness, which can lead to frustration and disappointment in the process of chanting.

Neophyte chanters are advised to hear the holy name with attention. They are asked to chant attentively from the start and from the heart. We all can recall our first attempts to perform Japa using prayer beads. I was told, "just chant and hear the mantra". Nevertheless, for me, "just hear the mantra" was not sufficient instruction. My attention quickly became lost in thought with sporadic, vague awareness of the mantra at best. Boredom and frustration soon followed. On hindsight, I desperately needed more instruction and training to develop the skill of chanting the mantra with attentive awareness. Those who are new to mantra meditation (as well as, old timers like me), can benefit from specific guidance and training in the art of chanting with an emphasis on staying present, not only while chanting, but also the practice of choosing to be present in daily life.

Unless the yogi learns to consciously direct attention within, find satisfaction in the self (atmavan) and observe the monkey mind with equanimity, it is difficult for most people - no matter how devoted they are - to hear and chant the Holy Name consistently with ease and attention. There are rare exceptions, of course! For those advanced yogis who already have spontaneous attraction for the holy names, awareness training is irrelevant. Such advanced souls have realized that the true self has no past or future and eternally exists in the present. For the awakened soul, being fully attentive to the Holy Name is as natural and spontaneous as the attraction young boys and girls experience for each other.

Those who begin chanting but don't experience the inner transformation they expected, understandably lose enthusiasm for chanting over time. Some discouraged practitioners eventually give up the practice of mantra meditation altogether. Other Bhakti yogis that find themselves in the same boat of dissatisfaction are able to continue the practice of mantra meditation, but they give up trying to chant with attention and resign themselves to chanting in a distracted and painfully bored state of mind for years on end. I can relate to their doubts and frustration because I also faced similar difficulties in the first twenty years of my practice of mantra meditation.

# References and Gratitudes

## Who is Srila Prabhupada?

"He was a genuine holy person with enormous integrity and compassion, and he had a powerful impact on those who met him. He never claimed authority and respect for himself; what he said and did was always in the name of Krishna"– Dr. Thomas J. Hopkins

His Divine Grace Srila A.C. Bhaktivedanta Swami Prabhupada is the founder acharya of ISKCON. On 17th September 1965, he entered the port of New York City to fulfil the desire of his Spiritual Master; which was, to spread holy names of Krishna in the western world. His mission was a huge success. He established 108 ISKCON temples, ashrams, and cultural centres around the world.

Abhay Charan Bhaktivedanta Swami Srila Prabhupada was born in a Hindu family on September 1, 1896. He was growing up in the British-ruled India. After a few years, he joined the civil non-cooperation movement started by Mahatma Gandhi for the freedom of the country. In 1922, he met his Spiritual Master Shri Srila Bhaktisiddhanta Saraswati Thakur, a well-known religious leader and scholar. The influence of Srila Bhaktisiddhanta Saraswati's philosophy proved to be a milestone in Abhay Charan's life. He told Abhay Charan to introduce the philosophies of Lord Krishna to the west. In 1933, he became a follower of Srila Bhaktisiddhanta. Later, he spent 32 years of his life in the preparation of his journey to the western countries to obey his guru's wish.

At the age of 69, he started his journey to New York City with only 40 INR in his pocket, a trunk full of books and some of his personal belongings on a cargo ship, Jalduta.

During the next 11 years, he circled around the entire world 14 times. He conveyed the teachings of Lord Krishna to countless people across six different continents.

The most imperative contribution of Srila Prabhupada are his books. He wrote more than 70 volumes on the tradition of Krishna. All the volumes are highly appreciated by the scholars because of their depth, clarity, and faithfulness towards the tradition. His work has also been used by several colleges in the form of textbooks. His books have been already translated into 76 different languages. His most appreciated and famous works include 'Bhagavad Gita As It Is', 30-volumes of 'Srimad Bhagavatam', and 17-volumes of 'Sri Caitanya- caritāmṛta'.

## Who is Lord Caitanya?

Sri Caitanya Mahaprabhu exhibited the highest level of devotion to Supreme Lord Sri Krishna. He is none other than the Supreme Lord Sri Krishna, who appeared in this Kali-yuga to inaugurate the yuga dharma for this age – "Sankirtana Yagya", the congregational chanting of the Holy Names of the Lord.

Sri Caitanya Mahaprabhu appeared at Sridhama Mayapura, in the city of Navadvipa in Bengal, on the Phalguni Purnima evening in the year 1486 AD. His father, Sri Jagannatha Mishra, a learned brahmana from the district of Sylhet, came to Navadvipa as a student. He lived on the banks of the Ganges with his wife Srimati Sachidevi, the daughter of Srila Nilambara Chakravarty, a great learned scholar of Navadvipa.

Their youngest son, who was named Vishvambhara, later became known as Nimai Pandita and then, after accepting the renounced order of life, Sri Caitanya Mahaprabhu.

The Lord left only eight slokas of His instructions in writing, and they are known as the Siksastaka. All other literatures based on His teachings were extensively written by the Lord's principal followers, the six Gosvamis of Vrindavana, and their followers.

His mission was to preach the importance of chanting the holy names of the Lord in this age of Kali (quarrel). In this present age, quarrels take place even over trifles, and therefore the shastras have recommended for this age a common platform for realization, *viz.* chanting the holy names of the Lord.

*harer nāma harer nāma harer nāmaiva kevalam*
*kalau nāsty eva nāsty eva nāsty eva gatir anyathā*

'In this Age of Kali there is no other means, no other means, no other means for self-realization than chanting the Holy Name, chanting the Holy Name, chanting the Holy Name of Lord Hari.'

Lord recommends always chant this mantra and be happy.

*Hare Krsna Hare Krsna, Krsna Krsna Hare Hare*

*Hare Rama Hare Rama, Rama Rama Hare Hare*

## *Chengdu association lectures on the morning and afternoon, May 6th, 2019.*

***An audio version of these lectures is also accessible on the following weblink: http://bhaktishastra.com/on-chanting-presence-and-releasing/***

Each of Prabhupada's disciples has their own personal experience with Prabhupada that directly informs their understanding of Krishna Consciousness and how they share their experience with others. The personal experience we have had with our spiritual master is reflected in the way that we - as individuals - communicate the teachings of Krishna Consciousness to others.

Some of my God brothers and sisters are focused on specific aspects of ISKCON's broad variety of services, which have a unified aim to spread the teachings of Lord Caitanya. For example, there is the ministry of education, temple construction, cow protection, book distribution, devotee care, writing, hospice care and such other forms of outreach.

Since Srila Prabhupada asked me to teach Krishna Consciousness in Japan, my service is focused in Asia. I personally witnessed Prabhupada's deep compassion for devotees who struggle to awaken in themselves

Krishna Consciousness; I also struggled for many years to chant and be happy. As a result of my experience in this regard, I am passionate about assisting devotees who, for one reason or another, are not feeling happy in Krishna Consciousness. I feel compassion for devotees who can honestly admit that they are unhappy even after many years of sincere practice of Krishna Consciousness. This teaching on Presence and Releasing is especially for such devotees who want to truly chant and be happy.

I know that not everyone can resonate with the way I present Krishna Consciousness. Some devotees cannot relate at all. That is okay, because, we are eternal individuals and everyone is at different stages on the evolutionary spiral of consciousness. I know my style is a little unorthodox. Some persons are only receptive to specific language terms and references when hearing about the absolute truth. When the language and concepts used are unfamiliar or outside the realm of one's tribe or tradition, it is understandable that they become confused or even get turned off by what they hear.

Really, terms and phrases such as Presence, I am spirit, I am not the body, Mindfulness, self-realization, Brahmabhuta, Atmavan, being situated in the self, etc. are different words describing the same state of consciousness. Therefore, misunderstandings can arise because of the different terminology used by different teachers and traditions to describe the awakened state of being.

For one reason or another, some devotees are not open to the teachings of Presence and Releasing as I present it, even though choosing to live in the present; or, even though the practice of mindful awareness is a basic principle on the path of spiritual awakening and Bhakti. To bring conscious attention to the present is taught in all bona fide spiritual traditions. Yet, this elementary step in spiritual awakening is often missed or over looked by overzealous spiritual seekers. Everyone in the Hare Krishna movement is taught from the beginning, *just chant and hear*. In other words, chant the mantra with attention. Be present when you chant.

The teaching of Presence and Releasing is not different from or opposed to Bhakti. Presence and Releasing support the cultivation of Bhakti. Understanding one is not the body, and chanting God's name with attention, are foundational practices of Bhakti yoga that can only be accomplished when attending to the present.

One begins Bhakti when faith in God appears in one's consciousness. The light of faith in God is compared to the tiny seed of a plant. When the seed is planted in soil and given water, it sprouts and begins to grow and mature.

The devotee places the seed of Bhakti in the soil of humility within the heart. With due attention, the devotee waters the Bhakti seed every day, with the sound vibration of the Holy Name. The devotee gardener is careful to identify and remove weeds of material desire whenever they pop up next to the Bhakti plant. If that is not done, the weeds of material desire may grow and eventually choke the Bhakti plant.

Attentive chanting directs the water of the Holy Name on to the Bhakti plant for nourishment. Attention is synonymous with Presence. Presence allows the devotee to be able to observe and extract weeds of material desire that spring up in the garden of the heart. When a devotee chooses to be present for the Holy Name, the Bhakti plant directly receives the water of the Holy Name. If material desires for name and fame arise, it is from the vantage point of present moment consciousness that the devotee can detect the weed and remove it. Releasing is the process of introspecting within the garden of the heart, bringing to consciousness illusory material desires and letting go of identification with the false self. As they say in AA (Alcoholics Anonymous), *Let go and let God*.

In my experience, many devotees are not sufficiently taught the spiritual basics of chanting with attention, or as I like to say, being present for the Holy Name. Neophyte devotees are properly instructed to hear the name with attention, which is correct. However, for me, "just hear" was not sufficient instruction. I certainly needed more training when it came to developing the skill of chanting attentively and the giving up of the material concept of life. In my opinion, most neophyte devotees could benefit from specific guidance and training in the art of focused chanting and introspection.

Furthermore, it is my contention that if from the very beginning of entrance into Bhakti-yoga, the likelihood of a devotee's ability to peacefully chant and be happy would greatly improve if devotees were systematically taught the art of Presence and releasing. Unless one learns how to be situated in the self (atmavan) and observe the monkey mind, it is difficult for most devotees to hear and chant the Holy Name consistently, with rapt attention. If a devotee lacks present moment awareness and cannot be present for the Holy Name, it is possible that a devotee may not experience the desired result of inner happiness that he/she expects from the practice of mantra meditation. This is often the case for those who begin chanting but then give up after some time.

We all want to be truly happy and in love with Krishna.

Sadly, I often meet devotees who tell me that they are not happy and that Japa is a struggle for them. They say that they don't truly enjoy chanting Japa even after years of sincere practice and service. They also tell me that they do not feel like they are progressing in Krishna Consciousness and they do not understand the reason for their lack of progress. I can relate to their doubts and frustration because I also faced similar difficulties in my spiritual life.

Most neophyte devotees are simply instructed, "Just chant and hear the mantra." In order to "Just chant and hear", you really have to be *here* consciously and nowhere else. You have to be present for the mantra, for Krishna, who is personally present in the sound of His Holy Name. When I emphasize being present, just being here for the Name is really all that I am suggesting. Yet some devotees still misunderstand my words and assume that I am speaking some doctrine that is outside our Caitanya Vaishnava tradition.

Of course, if my words create misunderstanding among some devotees that may also be due to my defect as a teacher. I am always attempting to improve and find effective ways to communicate spiritual concepts. The concept of presence cannot be understood by the mind because Presence is transcendent of the mind. It is only by the direct experience of presence that one can know definitively what I am talking about. At most, what words can do is to guide you to perform the work that will give you the experience that they (the words) are pointing to.

Therefore, we have created the two-day seminar and the five-day retreat to facilitate the experience of awakening in the present. For those devotees who are listening to this talk on Presence and chanting, I highly encourage you to participate at least once in the two-day seminar and the five-day retreat.

For some devotees, this teaching on Presence and Releasing may not be necessary. In this movement, there are devotees who come to Krishna Consciousness when they are already self-realized. Such awakened devotees intuitively understand that thoughts are not real. They know that the truth of life only exists now. These awakened devotees automatically live in the present and pay no attention to thoughts of past and future. Actually, one has to live in the present. Whatever is past is gone beyond recall, and, the future has not yet arrived. The self-realized devotee knows that remembering the past or imagining the future are only important to the extent that they help one deal with the present. Such awakened devotees are rare. The self-realized devotee is already spontaneously attracted to the Holy Name of Krishna.

This teaching of awakening, which we call Presence and Releasing, is actually basic level knowledge in all bonafide spiritual traditions – both, pluralistic and monistic.

Although rare, there are devotees who just come into this life already very advanced in Krishna Consciousness. Practically speaking, from the very beginning of joining this Hare Krishna movement, they fully realize they are not the body or mind. From the moment these advanced souls begin chanting, they are totally absorbed in the sound vibration of the Holy Name. So, at a deeper level they already understand the world of the mind is illusory. They therefore disregard thoughts. They know that to awaken out of the illusory world of the mind, one has to live fully in the present.

Since these devotees are spiritually awake, they directly perceive the truth that there is no life or reality outside of the present. Being spiritually awake, they already know this foundational truth of reality. After all, the tenth offense in chanting is inattention. Unless you are present for Krishna when you chant, chanting is offensive. If you are not 'here' when you chant, then where are you?

From my personal experience in the movement, I know that such advanced devotees do exist. I can personally testify that some of my God-brothers were already advanced in Krishna Consciousness from the first day they entered this movement. I have lived with them, talked with them, served with them day and night for years. I could observe in their words and behaviour that they were transcendentally situated in Krishna Consciousness.

So, for such devotees who already have spontaneous attraction for the Holy Name, this teaching on Presence and Releasing is irrelevant and not needed. But for devotees who do struggle to chant with attention and who honestly can say, *"I am not happy. I am still identified with this mind and body"* - for these devotees, this teaching on Presence and Releasing will be very beneficial if they choose to apply it in their life.

Actually, steady happiness is a sign of advancement in chanting and Bhakti. Here is an interesting quotation from a letter Srila Prabhupada wrote in 1973:

## *Three stages of Chanting*

*The three stages of chanting are, first to clean the mirror of the mind. Then the next stage, when the mind is cleansed, one becomes free from the symptoms of material existence. The third stage is: "He never laments nor desires to have anything; he is equally disposed to every living entity. In that state he attains pure devotional service unto me."*

*Letter to Susan Beckman -- Herts, England August 29, 1973: The chanting is a process of purification. Just like we use soap to cleanse the body, this is material, but the chanting is spiritual cleansing. The three stages of cleansing are first to clean the mirror of the mind. In the Bhagavad Gita it is said, "The mind is the best friend and the worst enemy. For one who has learned to control the mind it is the best of friends but for one who has failed to do so it is the worst enemy." Due to long term association, the mind absorbed in material things has become contaminated, or dirty; the chanting process purifies the mind. Then the next stage, when the mind is cleansed, one becomes free from the symptoms of material existence. Material existence means to be always hankering and lamenting. I must have a new automobile, I must have more money, I must have good wife, I must have this, I must have that. Then when I have the thing, I lament, I have lost my wife, I have lost my money, I have lost my car, simply lamenting. So, the second stage is to be free from this anxiety.*

## ***The third stage is:***

*Brahma-bhutah prasannatma*
*na socati na kanksati samah*
*sarvesu bhutesu mad*
*bhaktim labhate param*

*"He never laments nor desires to have anything; he is equally disposed to every living entity. In that state he attains pure devotional service unto me." (Bhagavad Gita 18.54*)

I would like to read from the Caitanya-caritāmṛta today. This is the section in the Madhya-Lila where Lord Caitanya instructs Sanatana Goswami.

When Lord Caitanya was 24 years old, he took sanyas. He left Mayapur and went to Jagannath Puri. The Lord resided on this planet for a total of forty-eight years. After He moved to Jagannath Puri, He travelled. From

His home base of Jagannath Puri, the Lord spent six years traveling around India. This period of the Lord's pastimes is called the Madhya-lila. After traveling around India, the Lord returned to Jagannath Puri and never left Puri again. Continuously for eighteen years, the Lord lived in Puri until He disappeared from this world at the age of forty-eight.

This portion of the Caitanya- caritāmṛta is called the Antyalila.

So Mahaprabhu was traveling to Vrindavan and on His way, the Lord stopped and stayed for some time in the city of Varanasi, which is located on the banks of the Ganga. It was in Varanasi that the Lord met with Sanatana and Rupa Goswami and instructed them in the science of Krishna Consciousness.

Varanasi is situated near another famous place called Triveni Sangam, meaning where three rivers join together. There is a festival held at Triveni Sangam every year in January called the Magmela and every twelve years called the Kumba Mela. Varanasi is located about half way between Vrindavan and Jagannath Puri. So, the Ganges, the Yamuna and the Sarasvati join together at Triveni Sangam. Varanasi is close by and the city of Allahabad is also very close-by. Prabhupada lived in

Allahabad for some years when he was a householder. The Lord Caitanya visited Allahabad as well.

It is very auspicious to bathe in the Ganga at this spot called Triveni at the designated auspicious time in the month of

January. This spiritually favourable festival at Triveni is called Magh (Month of January) Mela (festival). At Triveni, every 12 years in the month of Magh, there is a very special auspicious festival called Kumbha Mela. It is said that, if you bathe in the Ganga at Triveni during the Kumbha Mela at the correct astrological moment, you will go to Vaikuntha after leaving this body. So that very auspicious event occurs every 12 years.

I was fortunate to go to the Kumbha Mela in 1977 with Srila Prabhupada and a small number of his disciples. That year was the first time ISKCON had a presence at the Kumbha Mela. Every spiritual group, including all the yogis that have been living in caves in Himalaya and millions of other people are especially eager to attend the Kumbha Mela. For a few days, the river bank on the Ganges at Triveni becomes a city of tents full of millions of people. Many people from all over India and beyond go to the Kumbha Mela to bathe in the Ganga at the right time, seeking to achieve liberation.

The year I attended the Kumbha Mela was especially auspicious and is called Maha-Kumbha-Mela. The Maha-Kumbha-Mela occurs once every 144 years. From ISKCON's point of view, the Kumbha Mela is a great opportunity to preach and perform Sankirtan.

So Prabhupada wanted ISKCON to have a lecture and a preaching tent strategically located at the Kumbha Mela. But because it was ISKCON's first time at the Kumbha Mela, ISKCON's presence was not organized well. ISKCON was not able to obtain a central location. As a result, very few people were was coming to the ISKCON tent to see Prabhupada. So, Prabhupada intelligently decided to send his disciples out into the crowds, to perform Harinam sankirtan.

Going out on Sankirtan at the Kumbha Mela was very interesting. In those early days of ISKCON, majority of Prabhupada's disciples were white, fair-complexioned Americans. There were very few Indian followers of Srila Prabhupada. In our Sankirtan Party there were only two Asians devotees and a few black devotees; everyone else was Caucasian. So, we really stood out. Daily we went out on Harinam and this was a marvellous way to see the whole Kumbha Mela. There were many yogis at the Kumbha Mela who wore no clothes, in spite of the chilly weather. Many yogis had long matted hair and their bodies were covered in ash.

I remember getting up early every morning at around 2:30 am. to take a bath in the Ganga. From our camp site the Ganga was about 1-2 kms walk in the sand. After bathing and returning to our tent, I couldn't feel my feet; they had become so cold.

In the 1970s in India, there was no bottled water and the lack of clean water caused many devotees to become severely ill with dysentery, etc., Life at the Kumbha Mela was quite austere. According to my memory, there was Khichri to eat and it had sand in it. There were also rotten guavas and nothing else. Yet, we were ecstatic. We were young. Due to the daily Sankirtan party, gradually people started coming to see Prabhupada, so he was happy. However, after a few days in the cold climate of north India, in January, Prabhupada fell ill as well.

Prabhupada never quite recovered his strength and in the same year, about 8 months later, he left his mortal body.

Since all the people attending the Kumbha Mela wanted to bathe in the Ganga at the same appointed auspicious time, the Indian army had been deployed to keep peace and order. The Indian Army was in charge of crowd control. The Prime Minister of India at that time was Indira Gandhi; she also attending the Maha-Kumbha-Mela. There were thousands of Shaivites trying to enter the Ganga all at the same time. They were very fierce looking and the Indian Army had to keep them separate from others in the crowd. Historically, sometimes at the Kumbha Mela there were riots and different religious sects injured and killed each other in an attempt to bathe in the Ganga at the designated auspicious moment.

Anyways, sorry, I got off track. I beg your pardon. Now back to Lord Caitanya and his meeting with Rupa Goswami. Mahaprabhu instructed Rupa Goswami for ten days and Santana for three months at Varanasi. It is said that just as Krishna manifested the knowledge of Vedas within the heart of Lord Brahma, similarly Lord Caitanya manifested the knowledge of the science of devotional service within the hearts of Sanatana and Rupa Goswami. That was only 500 years ago; and, we have all the instructions that the Lord gave them contained right here in the Caitanya Caritamrita and the Nectar of Devotion.

In Madhya-līlā 19.151, Lord Caitanya speaks to Sanatana. Madhya-līlā describes Mahaprabhu's life during the six years that he travelled around India after entering the renounced order of life.

Ādi-līlā describes the period of time the Lord lived in Mayapur from his birth until he took sanyasa and left home to live in Jagannath Puri.

Madhya-lila talks about the six years the Lord travelled around India from His home base of Jagannath Puri after He took sanyasa. Antya-līlā depicts the last eighteen years of Lord Caitanya's life while he was living in Jagannath Puri. During the last eighteen years of the Lord's life, He never left Jagannath Puri again.

I want to share a famous verse spoken by Lord Caitanya to Sanatana Goswami that explains the process of how a conditioned soul awakens from the dream of Maya by the grace of Krishna and Guru, and eventually goes to live in the spiritual dimension. By the grace of Krishna and Guru, the conditioned soul receives the seed of Bhakti or faith in God.

It is an interesting question. How does a conditioned living-being awaken faith in God, Krishna? And then once we have faith in God, how are we supposed to nourish and cultivate this faith in God? Faith in God is the Bhakti plant that will eventually produce the fruit of pure love for God when the Bhakti plant reaches maturity.

*brahmāṇḍa bhramite kona bhāgyavān jīva*
*guru-kṛṣṇa-prasāde pāya bhakti-latā-bīja*

CC Madhya 19.151

In sacred literature, the seed of Bhakti is called Bhaktilatā-bīja. Bhakti means devotion, latā means creeper, and bīja means seed. All plants grow from a seed. First there's a seed, then it sprouts, and then it becomes a mature plant with fruits. It's funny, because all types of plant seeds look very similar and sprout with two tiny leaves. A seed cracks open with the introduction of water and will first produce a sprout with two small leaves. But all sprouts look so similar that one may not be sure of what kind of plant the sprout will become.

Lord Caitanya says: *"According to their karma, all living entities are wandering throughout the entire universe. Some of them are being elevated to the upper planetary systems, and some are going down into the lower planetary systems. Out of the millions wandering living entities, one who is very fortunate gets an opportunity to associate with a bona fide spiritual master by the grace of Kṛṣṇa. By the mercy of both Kṛṣṇa and the spiritual master, such a person receives the seed of the creeper of devotional service."*

In the purport to this verse, Prabhupada says that the Bhakti seed is the awakening of faith in God. By the grace of God and Guru, the fortunate human being receives transcendental knowledge regarding the truth of the soul and the truth of God. He comes to understand clearly that he is not God and that God, Krishna, is the Supreme Personality of Godhead, who is the cause of all causes. Faith in God arises out of having received this transcendental knowledge. Prabhupada also explains that the method given by spiritual master that awakens devotion to God is also considered an aspect of seed of faith in God, the seed of Bhakti.

Later on, in this section of the C.C., Mahaprabhu teaches that all devotees are expected to become gardeners of their Bhakti plant. By the mercy of God and Guru we have received the seed of pure devotion to God. As a gardener sows a seed, each devotee must sow the seed of Bhakti they received from their Guru in the soil of their heart. Seeds need to be placed in soil. Ideally the soil is rich in nutrients. The Bhakti seed grows best in the fertile soil of humility.

Sowing the seed of Bhakti in our heart is just the beginning. Protection, proper soil, frequent watering, sunlight and continuous weeding in the garden are all required for the Bhakti plant to grow and bear fruit. Until the seed has sprouted, grown and bears the fruit of love for God, the devotee must carefully water, protect and nurture the Bhakti plant. In fact, Mahaprabhu says that as long as we remain in the material world with a material mind and body, the watering process of chanting must continue, otherwise the plant may shrivel up and die.

What is required for a seed to sprout, grow and bear fruit? Sunlight, water, rich soil, protection from weeds and destruction by large animals are all essential for a plant to mature. All these items are necessary for the plant to grow, remain healthy and produce flowers and fruits.

Mahaprabhu has compared water and light to the chanting of the Holy Name. Giving up the material concept of life and all the material desire that are born out of this ignorance, Mahaprabhu has compared to pulling weeds.

Suitable soil is a prerequisite to planting a seed. Nutrient rich soil ensures that the seed has the necessary food to grow. According to Lord Caitanya, the qualities of humility, tolerance, respect for others and self-esteem creates the richest soil in which the seed of Bhakti can flourish. In His Shikshashitaka, Mahaprabhu has stressed the cultivation of the personal qualities of humility, tolerance, respect for all living beings and releasing the craving to be respected, as the qualification for entering into the mystery of the Holy Name. Lord Caitanya teaches in the third verse of his eight prayers that the cultivation of humility, tolerance, having respect for others and requiring no respect for oneself are character qualities the devotee must develop in order to experience a taste for chanting the Holy Name. In this context, humility, tolerance, respect for others, and being devoid of the need to be respected, are the elementary ingredients of the soil that best supports the seed of Bhakti as the seed grows. Humility naturally arises in a devotee who is courageously honest. Therefore, honesty that can penetrate the illusions arising from personal bias is also indispensable for the healthy growth of the Bhakti plant.

Of course, you can sow a seed anywhere and everywhere. You can leave a seed on a rock, or in sand. If you water the seed, the seed may sprout and grow a bit, but not very well; because, the roots cannot stabilize and there is not sufficient nourishment. Therefore, in order to grow a strong and healthy Bhakti plant, the soil of humility, tolerance, respect for all, and freedom from the need to be recognized by others are critical aspects of the serious practice of mantra yoga.

What is more important in the growth of a plant - rich soil, water, sunlight, weeding or a protective fence? Well, all are equally crucial.

In the above verse spoken by the Lord to Sanatana Goswami, the seed of Bhakti, faith in God, comes into this world and reaches the fortunate conditioned soul via devotees of the Lord in the form of the spiritual master. According to Adi-lila 1.34-35 and purports, there are different kinds of spiritual masters: the Guru who first tells you about Krishna; the Guru who gives you transcendental knowledge and instructions about the practice of Krishna Consciousness; and the Guru who initiates you. All these Gurus are considered to be equal and direct manifestations of Krishna's mercy. Normally, the person who initiates you (Diksha-guru) is first your instructor (Shiksha-guru). This is the normal course of awakening from the dream of Maya because it is by hearing about the absolute truth from one who has realized the truth, that one is able to develop faith in Guru and in Krishna as the cause of all causes and the ultimate goal of life.

Faith in Guru naturally develops when you first hear the Guru's words and observe his behaviour. Then, there is the person from whom you first heard about Krishna and his teachings. That person is also considered to be your Guru and a bona fide representative of Krishna. Krishna chose this devotee as a vehicle to introduce Himself to you. If you have the eyes to see, you can accept the devotee who first introduced you to Krishna Consciousness as your vartamapradaksha guru.

So, there are no accidents, right? Krishna is in the heart and can see when a particular conditioned living being is ready to awaken from the dream of separation from God and go back to Godhead. The Lord in the heart then makes that *Jiva-atma* (individual living being) fortunate by arranging for the *jiva-atma* to come in contact with a pure devotee and hear transcendental knowledge.

Transcendental knowledge is the knowledge about absolute truth, which is accurate knowledge about three subjects. There is truth of the *Jiva-atma*, of truth the absolute Godhead, the Isvara (Supreme controller) and the true way of liberation from the cycle of birth and death and the process to go back to Godhead.

The conditioned soul has been going round and round in this material world since time immemorial. We want answers to some important questions. How to come out of the mind and awaken? How to come out of the illusion of separation from God and break this cycle? How to become free from ignorance?

All of us know that special devotee who came into our life and introduced us to Prabhupada's teachings about Krishna and the Mahamantra. Krishna introduced Himself to us through that particular devotee. The person who firsts tells us about Krishna and His teaching is called the Vartamapradaksha guru.

As for me, I came to know of Krishna Consciousness when I met the devotees performing Harinam Sankirtan in the streets of Ginza, Tokyo in 1970. I joined the Harinam and afterwards the devotees in the Harinam party invited me to come back with them to the temple. The first person who really talked to me about the philosophy of Krishna Consciousness, was Tamal Krishna Goswami. I really liked the way he presented the teaching. Perhaps even more importantly, I also felt that he actually cared about me. Tamal Krishna left Tokyo with Prabhupada about a week later and went to India. I was especially impressed by Tamal Krishna Prabhu (he was married at that time) because he didn't forget about me. For next couple of months, he wrote me letters of encouragement. His letters would be full of kindness and really helped me continue on in Krishna Consciousness. So, I consider him to be my vartamapradaksha Guru.

The day after I talked with Tamal Krishna Goswami, I was fortunate to meet Srila Prabhupada. Intuitively, I knew immediately that Srila Prabhupada was my teacher sent by Krishna to deliver me from this material world. But also, please consider this; unless the devotees had gone out to Ginza on Harinam, I may have never gotten the opportunity to hear about Krishna or meet my spiritual master. So, every devotee is very, very special. Every devotee is representing Krishna, and people find out about Krishna through you. So, you are Krishna's instruments. Krishna is using all of you and you are representing Him. You are touching the hearts of others with the transcendental sound vibration that is coming from the spiritual world. In so many ways, you are encountering others and giving them the seed of Bhakti, faith in Krishna. On the Internet, WeChat, books and so many other ways, you are working hard to share KC with others.

## The second section: Afternoon

*kintu yadi latāra saṅge uṭhe 'upaśākhā'*
*bhukti-mukti-vāñchā, yata asaṅkhya tāra lekhā*

*"Sometimes unwanted creepers, such as the creepers of desires for material enjoyment and liberation from the material world, grow along with the creeper of devotional service. The varieties of such unwanted creepers are unlimited.*

CC Madhya 19.158

In this verse, the Lord explains that each devotee chanting Hare Krishna is responsible for the care and maintenance of the Bhakti creeper. Sometimes unwanted creepers grow in the vicinity of the Bhakti plant which is growing in the garden of our heart. These unwanted creepers are referred to as weeds. You have your Bhakti plant growing in your garden. You are watering the plant of devotion with the chanting of the Holy Names of the Lord.

In the previous verse, Mahaprabhu compares the chanting of the Holy Name to water given to the Bhakti plant. He says, we must make sure that the water is being poured directly on to our plant. Otherwise, if we are inattentive, the water of the Holy Name will go on to the weeds that surround the Bhakti plant. As a consequence of inattention, the weeds of the material concept of life will become nourished and strengthened. If inattention continues, we will never even notice the weeds of attachment to the bodily concept of life. Not only that; the weeds of material desire will grow and eventually choke the Bhakti plant.

If you are present (which means, chanting with attention) for the Holy Name, then you can be sure that the water of the Holy Name is nourishing your plant of devotion. On the other hand, if you are not present and are lost in the mind, lost in thought, just daydreaming as you chant, the water of the Holy Name will nourish the weeds of the false conception you have of yourself. The result is that you make very little progress in spiritual life even after many years of diligent practice.

Prabhupada says there is a simple test you can take in order to know if you are progressing on the path of Bhakti. Look within yourself honestly. Are you happy or not? You can know that you have made little or no progress in Bhakti if you find that you still lament the past and crave happiness in the future. If there is lack of inner happiness now, it is evident that you have yet to experience the truth of who you really are.

As you water your plant by chanting, unwanted weeds of material attachments spring up right next to the plant of devotion. Many different weeds come up and compete with the Bhakti plant for water and sunlight. Mahaprabhu is warning us to be on a lookout for these unwanted weeds so that we can identify them and pull them out.

Unless a certain level of Presence has awakened in you, how will you be able to look within and observe the weeds of the material concept of life? The false conception we have of ourselves is always competing with the Bhakti creeper and depriving the devotional plant of the light and water of the Holy Name. Unless we are present and attentive when chanting, we will not observe and notice when consciousness became lost in thinking.

On the contrary, when you are fundamentally awake in the present, you can easily observe when thoughts of material desire arise in the mind. In that moment of clear observation of the material desire, you have the opportunity to let it go. This is real detachment and weed extraction. Actually, it is only in the present that you can detach and let go of identification with any thought or material desire. Letting go of material desire is simply releasing consciousness from identification with thought.

The weeds are all varieties of material desires. The weeds of material desires originate from one source, which is the bodily conception of life. Due to ignorance, we imagine we are the material body and mind with a false sense of self. We imagine that we exist independent of God. As a result of this illusion, we feel separate from our true self and God. We feel incomplete and dissatisfied. Due to the underlying feeling of dissatisfaction, we look for love, acceptance and approval outside of ourselves, and ignore our eternal relationship with God. We look for others' approval in order to feel good about ourselves. We desire to enjoy the world without God. We desire liberation because we suffer in ignorance, not knowing our true self. Herein lies the great irony - the real "me" is non material, sat-cht-ananda. We already are what we are seeking!

In truth, we are already joyful and eternal beings of consciousness. We are searching in vain for fulfilment, not knowing that we already are complete. When you are awake in the present, you come out of the mind and the mind's unhappy story. When you are awake in the present, without effort, you feel complete and connected with the source of life. When you are present there is no desire for liberation. There is only a feeling of gratitude for your life and the source of life, Krishna.

Even the desire for liberation is considered a weed and is unfavourable for Bhakti. Pure Bhakti is devoid of selfish desires. Pure Bhakti is a desire to please Krishna in the way that is actually pleasing to Him.

There is no guessing or speculation allowed when it comes to knowing what is favourable and pleasing to Krishna. Guessing or speculating has no place in pure Bhakti. We know how to please Krishna by following in the footsteps of the previous Acharya. Also, Krishna Himself tells us in BG that pure Bhakti - devoid of selfishness - is the only way to please Krishna. Love for love's sake is the essence of the Bhakti lata bija.

So, as you water the Bhakti plant by chanting Hare Krishna, other creepers are also sprouting up. At first glance, all the creepers may look the same. So, the question arises, how to distinguish the pure Bhakti sprout from the sprout of material desire? The verse is telling us that the weeds are composed of many varieties of material desires. It is up to each one of us to scan the garden in our heart. Via introspection and honest observation, we will be able to distinguish the weeds of material desire from the Bhakti plant of pure desire to please the Lord. The sprout of pure devotion is free of (egoic) personal expectations for fame, distinction and adoration.

Thoughts are easily seen from present moment awareness. All material desires arise as thoughts projected onto the screen of the mind. Simultaneously, thoughts are reflected in the body as emotional and physical sensations. The mind detects the thoughts and feelings and thinks: "This thought and feeling is real and about *me and mine*", this is false ego. From awakened presence, you see the thoughts; you can choose to let them go and dis-identify with the false self. You can pull out the weed.

Material desire always arises from the false concepts that we have of ourselves. Our misidentification with the material mind and body, lies at the root of every material desire. Lord Caitanya is saying a devotee should introspect and alertly scan the garden of the heart to actively search for any material motivations. We must be present enough so that we can observe within and see if we are harbouring egotistical desires for recognition, acceptance and approval. The Lord is directing all devotees of the Holy Name to look within and observe the garden of the heart to see what kinds of plants are being cultivated there. Further, the devotee must be willing to exercise the proper use of free will by choosing to remove any weeds of material desire.

What are some more examples of material desire weeds? The verse says there are unlimited material desires. How about the desire to be special? Do you ever perform your devotional service with the expectation that everyone else should recognize and honour you for the service you do? Do you want to be respected, or to be acknowledged? You are doing Krishna Bhakti; maybe you are leading the kirtan, chanting Krishna's Names, but at the same time maybe you also have some hidden egoistic agenda, such as the thought that, *I hope everyone is going notice that I'm a great singer.*

Most of us quietly maintain in our heart the material desire to be special in the eyes of others. We all have a false ego that is desperately seeking love, acceptance and approval. Such ego desires are quite normal and we can even feel compassion towards the false ego when we see how fragile and afraid it is. Although you may indeed have such a desire for recognition as you perform service, unless you are intentionally on the lookout for material desires within, you may never even see them.

Many material desires exist in the form of unconscious thoughts, feelings and strategies for happiness in the future. Thought patterns rapidly appear and disappear on the screen of the mind. Egoistic thoughts arise constantly into the mind space and pass by mostly unnoticed. We are habitually thinking about what we want and don't want. If you are committed to living life awake in the present, you will be less likely to remain lost in the mind, daydreaming. From presence, you will be able to observe your ego's habitual patterns of thought and release your identification with your false-ego and thoughts.

Many people don't even know how to look within because they don't know where "within" really is. The world of the present reality is distinctly different than the world of the mind. Life in the present is real, whereas life in the mind, remembering the past and imagining the future, is false and has no basis in reality. For the yogi, understanding the clear distinction between thinking and awareness is foundational for spiritual awakening. The more one chooses to be present, the more one is able to realize the difference between thinking and awareness.

In truth, we cannot serve Krishna and attempt to satisfy the wants of our false ego at the same time, thinking "I am" the doer. That is not Krishna Bhakti. Material desire for fame, adoration and distinction are opposed to Pure Bhakti. Contrary to our ego's expectation, it is only pure Bhakti that can satisfy the true self, the eternal unit of consciousness.

Material desires, where do they come from? They are coming from our self-image - the person we imagine ourselves to be when we are lost in thought. Externally, we are performing Krishna Bhakti, but the inner motivation is to satisfy our false ego. The result is that the false ego gets maintained and the Bhakti plant doesn't get any nourishment. This is one reason we may be chanting for many years but really do not experience steady happiness within or significant inner transformation. Prabhupada once replied to a reporter's question that he was transforming *Hippies* to *Happies*:

When you are present, conscious awareness becomes magnified. From awakened presence, it is easy to look within and to detect and observe the desires of the false ego as they appear on the screen of the mind. When you are not present, consciousness is absorbed in thinking and identification with the false self is magnified. It is that simple. When you are present and chanting, the water of the Holy Name is nourishing the Bhakti plant. When you are chanting and thinking of past and future, the water of the Holy Name is nourishing the illusion of your false self.

Sometimes devotees mistakenly believe that if *I just chant*, material desires will disappear without need of any personal effort to observe them and to let them go. Yet, we all have free will. Do you really believe those materialistic creepers are just going to disappear as long as you unconsciously are holding on to them? Only you have the power to choose where you will place your conscious attention. When a material desire arises in your mind and body to enjoy the opposite sex and you become absorbed in thinking, you are maintaining that desire and identification with the false self. How will this material desire ever disappear?

On the other hand, if this desire for sex appears in mind and you observe it and let the thought/feeling go, that is an act of detachment and you have released consciousness from identification with the false self. It is also true that if you actually chant with attention, for that moment, you are no longer maintaining the material concept of life or material desires. In the present, Consciousness is pure.

These questions can be raised, *why do I remain in the bodily concept of life, in spite of diligently chanting for many years? Why is there still lamentation about the past and craving for happiness in the future? Why are the weeds of material desire – such as, wanting to be special - still growing within the heart?*

According to Lord Caitanya, it is up to each one of us to use our free will to locate the weeds and pull them out. At the very least, we have to be conscious enough to notice when the desire to be special arises in our mind, be willing to acknowledge the thoughts, and then, just for now, let go of the feeling of wanting to be special. Stay present and repeat as necessary. Then we can confess the thoughts and feelings of the false ego aloud and ask the Lord of the heart for help.

This is how we pull the weeds. We have to make the conscious choice to locate and remove the weeds. Just be willing to bring into the light of consciousness the weeds of material desire by noticing, acknowledging, and confessing thoughts of material desire as they arise in mind. This is the proper use of free will and surrender to the Lord. The Lord then helps us!

Most of us were never trained how to look within and how to identify the weeds of material desire and pull them out. To make matters worse, many of us when we chant, are unconsciously identified with thought and do not even know it. When we are chanting and also lost in thought, we are continuously pouring water on the weed of the illusory material concept of life. The false concept of yourself that imagines that *"I exist independent and separate from Krishna"*, is being maintained whenever you are chanting and daydreaming at the same time.

If we are not awake in the present, we never see the distinction between the real self that exists in the eternal now and the illusory self that exists in the past/future concocted world of the mind. Most people are so distracted and addicted to thinking, that it is impossible for them to notice the creepers of material desire growing in their heart next to the Bhakti creeper. Therefore, it would be very beneficial for devotees to receive training on how to be awake in the present and look within.

Devotees would then be empowered to observe thoughts without getting involved and lost in thought. When you are consciously able to observe thoughts and emotions from Presence, that creates some space between consciousness and the illusory thoughts and feelings. Continuously choosing to be present, makes space between consciousness and thought, and releases consciousness from identification with the mind and body.

Automatically and effortlessly, the devotee who is trained to live in the present will be able to notice when he is caught in the illusory world of the mind and let go. From presence, the devotee remains peaceful and steadily chants the Holy Name with gratitude and respect.

Lord Caitanya is instructing Sanatana Goswami, which means the Lord is also instructing us to observe the garden within us and identify and pull out the weeds of material desire. A healthy garden does not just grow and stay healthy without the gardener's attention and care. Careful observation of the garden is required if your Bhakti plant is to thrive. A garden must have a gardener.

When all of you first joined Krishna Consciousness, I am sure you were instructed, *"Just chant and be happy." "Just sit down, chant and listen to the mantra."* So, you and me, we all had that expectation: *I will chant and be truly happy at last,* right? Because we are all suffering, isn't that true? One reason people come to Krishna Consciousness is that they don't want to suffer anymore. Naturally, we want to awaken from a bad dream.

We are instructed that if you do this chanting, you will become happy; and, if we actually chant in the way Lord Caitanya has taught and prescribed, we will be happy. We will actually surrender to the Holy Name. We will stay attentive to the Holy Name and let go of material desire. In truth, our nature as living beings is joyful. As a unit of pure consciousness that is part of God, we are happy to be alive and to chant God's Holy Names. Chanting God's name is the perfection of life and our relationship with God.

The main reason we remain unhappy, in spite of years of diligent spiritual practices, is because we are still living in the past and future illusory world of the mind, where false self exists. We are yet to realize the distinction between thinking and awareness. Our waking consciousness is lost in thought and maintaining a false conception of who we are. Who we think we are, is not real; it is just a phantom of who we are in truth. The thought of who we are is not the truth of who we are. The person we imagine ourselves to be is only the unhappy "me" that laments the past and dreams of happiness in the future. We are still holding on to the false concept we have of ourselves.

Without having a certain degree of presence awakened in consciousness (being self-aware in the present moment), it is difficult for an aspiring devotee to distinguish the Bhakti creeper from the weeds of material desires. Without awakened presence, the power to introspect is weak. After all, we have been distracted by thinking for lifetimes.

Furthermore, the false ego very expertly masquerades as a devotee. Normally we believe, "Yes, I am doing this chanting or this service for Guru and Krishna. But on closer inspection we find that the false ego has become mixed up in our devotional service. The false ego has some need or agenda to be fulfilled from the activities of devotion, like wanting to be special in the eyes of others, wanting acceptance, or seeking to experience bliss. Therefore, from the beginning of our practice of Krishna Consciousness, it is vital for us to be absolutely honest and introspective. Otherwise, the false ego may take over our spiritual life and we won't even realise it.

There is a simple and effective solution for coming out of the illusory world of the mind and the domination of the false ego. Often during your day, make a conscious choice to be present with something present with you; become aware that you exist now; and, thank Krishna for your life. To be present is so simple that the false ego will dismiss being present as nothing special. Dismissing being alive in the present as *nothing special,* is one of the false ego's many deceptive tricks to keep you asleep and under its control. For, as soon as you become bored with the present, you start to seek what is next, and then consciousness is back in the mind and asleep dreaming of the future. But you can only be awake now. You can only experience your life and the joy of being *now*. You can only hear the Holy Name *now*. Happiness is only *now*.

To come out of illusion, you have to begin with what is real. The present is real and whatever exists in the present is also real. The is no in-between. You are either here and awake, or not here - which means you are in the mind dreaming. You are either experiencing life now, which is real, or you are thinking about your life, which is not real. Only you can choose.

All humans have free will to place conscious attention anywhere they want, anytime they want. Simply, choose to be present with something that is present with you. Be present with whatever you can see, hear, touch, smell or taste as you gently remember to be present as you go about your day. Gradually the present moment will reveal your true self as an eternal conscious being. The present will reveal your presence as a being of pure awareness.

When you are present with something that is present, like the Tulsi plant or your breath, consciousness must come out of the mind, because, the world of the mind is always about past and future. When you are present, there is only awareness of the object and of yourself as an aware being, who is witnessing the object. Thoughts stop automatically as you give your full attention to Tulsi-devi. When you are present, you are aware of what exists now without judgment. If interfering mental projections arise in the mind to distort the reality of life, you just label the judgmental thought as *Thinking.* Let the thought go and return to the present moment reality.

Choose to be present with your breath, or with the Tulsi tree, or the sound of the mantra. Immediately you come out of the mind and the false ego's *unhappy me* story. You are present with Tulsi. You are here. *Who is here? I am*. You are now conscious of being conscious. You are an awakened being for those moments you are present and aware of your presence. You have awakened out of the dream world of the mind into the reality of your true life, which can only be experienced now.

By making a conscious choice to observe Tulsi, Tulsi becomes the place where you can anchor your attention into the present moment. This is because seeing Tulsi cannot take place outside of the present moment. Whenever you are present, you are conscious; and whenever you are consciously present, it is there you perceive the awareness that you are. You are aware that you are alive now. Who is alive?

There is a silent knowing, *I am*. This silent knowing of *I am* is not a thought. This knowing that *I am*, is what is called the truth or reality of life. You are conscious of being conscious. Even if you are conscious of being conscious for only a few seconds in the beginning, that is okay. Gradually you will awaken spiritually if you are committed to living in the present.

The truth of who you are is that you are an unchanging, conscious being of awareness that is emanating from Krishna. You and I really have no separate existence apart from God. Imagining that *"I exist"* separate from the source of life, is just the dream of Maya. When you make a conscious choice to be present with something that is present with you, like the Tulsi plant for example, you awaken out of the dream of separation from God; at least for those moments you are self-aware in the present.

In my experience of practicing Krishna Consciousness over the last fifty years, I have met quite a few people who began the practice of Krishna Consciousness but stopped after some time. When I ask those people why they stopped chanting, I have heard a common reply. Many people have told me that the reason they gave up chanting was because in the beginning they had great hope of becoming happy by chanting but were never able to find the happiness they were seeking. So, after some time they gradually stopped chanting because they felt bored, frustrated and not happy. Eventually they decided to search elsewhere in the hope of finding satisfaction.

I have no doubt that most people who begin chanting are very sincere. Such people try their best to chant exactly as they were instructed by their teachers. They also do service, and diligently study Krishna's teachings. Yet, as time passes - it may be months or even years in some cases - eventually some people stop chanting and give up the path of Krishna Consciousness. Why is that?

Why do people stop chanting? A common reply to this question is to attribute a waning or lack of interest in Krishna Consciousness to offenses committed to the Holy Name while chanting, which may be true. But for whatever reasons, we can also conclude that those who stopped chanting probably never found the happiness they were looking for in the practice. Why would anyone give up something that gave them happiness?

Is it possible that people who give up chanting for one reason or another have not yet spiritually awakened and experienced the joy of being in relationship with the Supreme Being?

A common offense made while chanting is for the chanter to not be present or attentive to the sound of Krishna's name. If one doesn't feel happy while chanting, most probably he or she is daydreaming while chanting. When chanting, if the devotee is inattentive, consciousness is somewhere other than in the present hearing the Holy Name.

If not in the present, where is the consciousness then? Consciousness is lost in the illusory mental world of the mind. The illusory world of the mind is where the imagined unhappy self lives. As long as you chant inattentively, you won't be able to experience the truth of who you are as a pure, joyful, unchanging being of awareness. If you are not present, you are not capable of recognizing the difference between your true self and the illusory self that exists only in the past future world of the mind.

The false ego doesn't want you to be present ever, even when you chant. For, when you are present, the false ego is not present and the false ego doesn't like that. When you are present, the false ego is no longer in control of your life. The imaginary self is full of fear and doesn't like *not* being in control. No control equals fear in the illusory world of the false self.

The false ego would rather keep you seeking happiness in the future by checking out varieties of spiritual practice and hearing many lectures, etc., because when you are seeking, you are not present and consciousness is in the future world of the mind. To keep you in search of the next high is one of the false ego's most effective strategies to keep you lost in the mind. By keeping you seeking, the false ego can continue to dominate your life.

The false ego loves it when you want to try out this practice or that. The false ego enjoys hearing talks about future attainment and various other people's stories of enlightenment and bliss. The false ego even wants to understand intellectually the different states of consciousness that are possible to attain when you someday become enlightened. The false ego is always motivated by the hope of reaching perfection and happiness. Seeking enlightenment is futile, because, the false ego is just another feature of the mind. The mind is material and not conscious. Therefore, the egoistic mind will never be able to understand consciousness. Consciousness is beyond the mind. Only consciousness can understand consciousness by direct experience in the present.

As long as you are seeking, you are not here; you are in the mind somewhere other than here and the false ego remains in control of your life. The false ego thinks, *I will try this teaching to become enlightened or will try another method, which gives me hope of attaining salvation in the future*. So, as long as the false ego can remain hopeful or faithful, it will diligently perform sadhana and practice the methods. Indeed, the false ego can continue on like this for years as long as it receives a steady stream of inspiration from outside sources, or until the false ego becomes exhausted and doubtful. At this point, a devotee will give up or go deeper to discover the true self that is transcendent of the false ego.

The false ego does not actually want you to be awake and self-aware in the present, even though the false ego is interested in liberation. So, if you happen to discover the gateway to awakening out of the mind into the present moment, the false ego will do whatever it takes to obstruct you from living in the present.

It is easy to understand when you are in the mind because even though you are here physically in the present reality, consciousness is projected into the mind thinking about the past or the future, which is imaginary. When consciousness is lost in the mind, you want to be there or somewhere other than here, which is always past or future and not real.

The only way you can leave here, is to go into your mind and think your way out of here. You leave the present reality energetically whenever you are seeking, whether you are hoping for happiness or even enlightenment in the future. As soon as you are seeking, you are in the mind and the false ego has you under its patterns of control.

It is important to note that if you are *seeking* presence, you will not find it. When you are present, you are willing to be with whatever is present with you. You are simply self-aware in the present with whatever is present with you that can be perceived through your five senses. In the present, there is nothing to seek out or find. Seeking or trying to find what is presence, keeps you in the mind and blocks the experience of presence. Since you are *seeking* to experience presence, your consciousness is actually in the mind and having thoughts about what presence must be like.

To be present, you simply have to bring consciousness to the present and notice what is here with you in the present reality and to be conscious of being conscious in the now. You relax into the present by becoming conscious of whatever is present with you now. In this moment, what do you see, hear, feel? Who is seeing, hearing, feeling? I am. There is no seeking or doing to be present. Presence is just a choice you make to bring conscious attention to what is happening now. You are just here and self-aware in the present.

Persons who give up chanting most probably didn't really know how to be present for the Holy Name. They didn't apply the process of hearing and chanting properly from the beginning. Most likely, they never received the necessary instruction of how to actually be attentive to the mantra. I know, because at one time in my life I was one of these people. To chant effectively, you need to actually hear the mantra, and in order to hear the mantra you must be here and present to the sound of the mantra.

We also know devotees who had been Chanting Hare Krishna for thirty years or more and then suddenly they stop chanting. We are shocked; how could this happen? Well, this is the reason: Unless you discover your true self, which is only perceivable in the present, you will never find happiness within. Without being awake in the present, spiritual practices will fail to make you happy. Unless your attention is in the present as you chant, you will not actually hear the Hare Krishna mantra. Nor will you experience the joy of being. How long can one honestly continue to chant and at the same time feel unfulfilled, or worse, feel bored?

There really is nothing you need to do and nowhere you need to go in order to be what you already are, which is an eternal conscious being of joy. Paradoxically, we are seeking what we already are. Who you are is revealed to you in the present, because you are an eternal being. You, as an eternal being, have no past or future. You can only know yourself now.

When you chant with full awareness of who you are now, chanting becomes a way of expressing your gratitude to Krishna for the abundance of life He is giving to you now. In other words, you can chant with a pure motive to please Krishna without expecting anything more from Him. That is because you are aware that Krishna is already giving you life, and this life the Lord is giving you is already complete. Spontaneously, out of love, you want to give back.

Choosing to live in the present does not mean that thinking needs to stop. I am not suggesting that thinking should stop or that thinking is somehow opposed to spiritual awakening. To stop thinking is not possible. Nor is it necessary to stop thoughts in order to awaken spiritually and chant in ecstasy. The purpose of the mind is to think. You can live consciously in the present and still use your mind to think. You can still have a story. When thinking is required, for e.g., when you are at work, then think. But if thinking is not required, for e.g., when you are taking a walk, or chanting Hare Krishna, then rest consciousness in the present and enjoy just to ***be*** as you walk and chant.

Once you know what it means to live in the present, you can choose to either be present or think. The difference is that you no longer get lost in the mind, or in your story. Sooner or later, everyone must surrender to this simple truth. The truth is that life does not exist outside of the present. Once you know this truth, you can transcend the mind and the false ego's story. You no longer get lost because you no longer believe in the illusion of the past and future world of thought. The present reveals the truth of who you are and who you are not.

The thing is, if you are honest and sincerely want to know the truth, Krishna says in BG 10.10 that He will help you by lighting up your heart so that you can perceive the truth that is already within you. The Lord in the heart will shine the light within and dissipate the darkness for anyone who is consistently devoted to Him. If you keep chanting, Krishna will help you from within. The Lord, who exists at the centre of your being, will reveal to you the secret of awakening to the truth that exists within you.

The Lord of the heart will guide you and show you how to look within so you can observe the ever-changing flow of the mind and body. As soon as you are able to consciously observe thoughts and feelings that arise in the mind/body, consciousness is automatically released from the trance of identification. From inner observation, it becomes clear that the mind and body are constantly changing, but you (the consciousness) are not. By looking inside and observing thoughts and feelings, it also becomes clear that the "one" who is witnessing the changes of the mind and body is not changing. You begin to awaken. By your direct experience you can see that *you*, the presence of awareness, does not change and is fully complete and connected with the Lord of the heart.

From awakened presence, you can observe within and see with clarity any creepers in the garden of your heart that are opposed to pure Bhakti. The weeds that originate from the false material concept of life are easy to spot from the vantage point of the present moment. This clarity of vision is the gift of the Super-soul to the sincere soul who wants to know Him. The Lord of the Heart empowers you to identify and pull out the weeds of desire that are based on the illusions you have about yourself. You simply notice, acknowledge and let go of materialistic desires whenever you observe them and return to the truth of life in the present. If you truly want to give up the illusion that "I" exist separate from Krishna, Krishna will smile and give you a helping hand.

Here is the critical factor in the process of awakening out of illusion - all human beings are endowed with free will. It is up to you to decide to look within. It is only from the present that you can know by direct experience the distinction between the reality of your *true self,* that exists always in the present, and the *illusory self,* that appears like a phantom in the past / future world of the thinking mind.

It is only from the awakened state of consciousness, which is perceivable in the present, that you can witness and let go of the material concept of life and live from your true self. From presence, you can directly know the truth that *I am because God is. I am the eternal servant of Krishna.* The present reality is the only reality and it is always available to you, but you have to choose it.

Next verse:

*'niṣiddhācāra', 'kuṭīnāṭī', 'jīva-hiṁsana' lābha', 'pūjā',*
*'pratiṣṭhādi' yata upaśākhā-gaṇa*

*"Some unnecessary creepers growing with the bhakti creeper are the creepers of behaviour unacceptable for those trying to attain perfection, diplomatic behaviour, animal-killing, mundane profiteering, mundane adoration and mundane importance. All these are unwanted creepers.*

CC Madhya 19.159

It is especially important to be vigilant and recognize whenever the desire for adoration and distinction arises in the mind. How can you let go, or pull out a weed, unless you are first able to notice the weed and admit that the weed is your creation? The weed is growing in your garden.

Once you have noticed and admitted the desire for recognition whenever this desire arises in your mind, you can confess to the Super-soul *"Oh, Lord there it is. I have been wanting everyone to recognize the service I do and to praise me."* After you honestly confess, let it go.

In this endeavour, magical thinking and laziness are your enemies. By the term *magical thinking*, I mean to believe that desires based on the material concept of life are just going to magically disappear and that you don't need to make any effort to let them go. Without bringing the desire to be special and other types of ego desires into the light of your introspective consciousness, such egocentric desires will stay below the level of consciousness and take root and grow next door to your Bhakti-lata-bija.

To pull out the weeds of material desire is simple, but not always easy. First you need to be present enough to notice material desires when they surface in your mind as thought forms and, in your body, as emotional feelings. Then you have to intentionally feel the feeling in your body. Contained in the thought and desires is a feeling that is reflected in your body as a sensation.

For example, let us say you are angry because someone mistreated you in public. As you remember the incident, you picture in your mind's eye the person who hurt you and you also hear the words they said. Simultaneously, there arise emotional feelings of anger and shame in your body. Perhaps you feel a tightness in your head and chest area.

Thoughts contain feelings that are always reflected in the body as sensations. You may have happy thoughts, angry thoughts, worrisome thoughts and all thoughts have a feeling associated with them. Feelings basically fall into two categories of pleasure or pain. We crave pleasure and resist pain. Both, craving and resistance cause more pain and more identification with the mind and body. See BG 7.27

To pull the weed of material desire, you first need to acknowledge the egoistic thought of wanting to be special (for example) and then notice how your body feels. Bring your attention to the body and feel. When you want something and you don't have it, (if I want to be special, that means you actually don't see yourself as special) there will be subtle feelings of self-doubt with slight sensation of discomfort or a tightness, in the body. The feeling and thoughts are connected together. Both need to be brought to consciousness in order for you to be able to let go, or pull out the weed. You notice, acknowledge, feel the feeling, confess to the Lord and let go. Return to the present.

The mind is very tricky and can tell itself very convincing lies. For instance, you may be feeling angry, and everyone around you can see that you are angry. Yet, your ego may protest to one and all that "I am not angry". This is especially the case if you were taught as a child that being angry in public is socially unacceptable.

Trust your body. The mind may be sneaky but you can always trust your body. The body will tell you the truth. The body doesn't lie. If you are having an angry thought, the feeling of anger will always be reflected in the body as an uncomfortable feeling, as a tightness or contraction. The body will always alert you with a little red flag with an uncomfortable feeling, that says, *"You are off-course, you are not living in the truth of who you are. You are living in the illusion of who you are."* You can use the feeling in the body to alert you and help you locate the weeds of material desire that are growing in the garden of your heart. The practice of being present is a very embodied state. The more you choose to be present, the more in tune you will be with your body and be able to recognize the signals that the body is sending you.

To pull out the weeds of illusion, you bring the thought forms and feeling of material desire into consciousness by noticing the thoughts and feelings. Consciously and intentionally feel the feeling of contraction that accompanies the dissatisfaction of *wanting,* which is reflected in the body as a sensation. The skill of letting go develops when you can feel the feelings with an attitude of honest acceptance and without becoming lost in the story that the thoughts are telling you. The more you consciously observe thoughts and feelings and accept responsibility for them, confessing them to the Super-soul, without getting lost in your story, the better you become at this practice of weeding the garden of the heart. Just remember to honestly confess thoughts and feelings to the Super-soul and ask for His help.

Doing this yard work in your garden is an important part of the gradual process of awakening. All that is happening is that you are becoming conscious of what was previously going on unconsciously. You are becoming conscious of your unconscious patterns of conditioning. You are coming to higher consciousness, which is the stepping stone to advancement in Krishna Consciousness. Just remember to consciously feel the feeling in the body that is contained in your thoughts because it is your unconscious reaction to the feeling in the body that reinforces the illusion that thoughts are real. Identification with emotional feeling and sensations creates the delusion of duality that Krishna talks about in BG 7.27.

Thoughts and feelings are always about the past, which is gone, or the future, which has not arrived. Both are illusory, yet the feeling that the thoughts produce in the body are felt in the now. Even though you are here, when you remember the past or imagine the future, you feel like you are there. This is the duality of delusion, which binds and conditions the living being to the material mind and body. BG 7.27

*O scion of Bharata, O conqueror of the foe, all living entities are born into delusion, bewildered by dualities arisen from desire and hate.*

*Iccha-Dvesha, I want it. I don't want it.* The desire to be special and important are a combination of thoughts that have a feeling attached to them. There is a *feeling of wanting* and *dissatisfaction* in the body. There is also a dreadful feeling of self-doubt and fear that feels tight and uncomfortable. When you want what you don't have, there is feeling of painful dissatisfaction. In both cases - wanting or not wanting - there is suffering and discomfort. When we unconsciously react to these feeling with craving or aversion, the illusion of *I am this mind and body* deepens as well as the conditioned reactive pattern. The weeds keep growing.

There is a fantasy of wanting to be more than you actually are, and conversely the fear that you are not enough. When you want something, it means you don't have it. There is a feeling of lack, of not enough and a discomfort contained within the feeling of *wanting*. These conditioned thoughts and feelings are running our life just below the level of consciousness; and our job as gardeners is to bring them to consciousness for releasing.

## ***Steps for pulling out the weeds:***

So, the first step is to just honestly notice that there are thoughts about wanting "recognition" and to be "special", to be better than others, etc. Notice the thoughts of wanting to be special. With conscious intent, feel the sensation of *wanting* within the body. Then, admit to yourself, *"Oh, I see it, there is wanting to be special."* Finally, confess it all to the Super-soul within you that exists as the very source of your being.

'Confession' just means that you honestly speak to the Lord of the Heart and admit that you have this desire to be recognized as a great devotee or perhaps have another egocentric desire you want to express. You admit to yourself and to the Lord, *"I feel like ashamed. I secretly want to be adored, etc."* Then ask the Lord, *"Please help me to let go of these thoughts and feelings of wanting to be a great devotee. I want to let it all go. Thank you, Lord."* Repeat as necessary. Gradually you will become an expert gardener. You will become more and more skilled at introspection, at recognizing weeds, and keeping your garden clear of such weeds.

All the variety of creepers of material desire originate from the same source. The origin of material desire is ignorance of one's true Self and relationship with Krishna. If we don't know our true self, then we will not know our true value. If we don't know the value of our true self, we live with a false sense of self with concocted values. Many people suffer all kinds of fears and anxieties due to a low sense of self-worth. This false sense of self is a mentally constructed program we developed as children. This imagined "me" believes at its core that *I am not good enough*.

When consciousness is not self-aware in the present, by default consciousness is lost in identification with the imagined self that exists within the illusory world of the mind. When we are identified with thoughts, we experience a false sense of self. We have taken ourself out of the reality of the present moment and into the illusory world of the mind. We have become lost in the mind, habitually thinking about the past and future. When we are identified with thoughts, we believe in whatever ideas the false self, the false ego, is telling us. We remain caught in our story, life after life -attempting to prove to ourselves and to everyone around us that *I am good enough*, even though we believe in the mentally programmed illusion from our childhood that says, *I am not good enough.* This *I am* is the mentally constructed *I am* not the real ***I am***, of course.

Before spiritual awakening, your home is the illusory - Past / Future - world of the mind, which is where the false self exists and is in control. You live in your story, which is everything from the past and everything in the future. But when you are self-aware in the present, you come out of the illusory story. You come out of that dream self, with all of its insecurities. When you bring conscious attention to the now moment, you are conscious of being conscious and awaken to your true self, at least for the moments you are self-aware in the present. In the now, there is no fear, no lack, no story - just alert awareness of being alive.

And what is in the story? Your story goes all the way back to your childhood. Your story includes and is based upon misconceptions about yourself that you acquired as a small, dependent child. These false beliefs about yourself were formed in your early childhood.

Examples of common false beliefs about ourselves that we all share are:

*I am not good enough. I cannot do it. I am no good. I am not loved. There is no one here for me. I am all alone. No one loves me or cares about me. I don't deserve to be loved. I am bad. I am no good. Everyone hates me. I am fat and not lovable. I am too stupid. I don't deserve to live.*

Once those limiting beliefs are programmed into your mind, they determine your experience of life. Unless you are on a genuine spiritual path and awaken from the dream world of the mind by discovering your real life in the present, most people remain in a dream state of consciousness, even when their eyes are open and they appear to be awake.

The mind identified, un-awakened person, maintains these false beliefs and misconceptions about themselves until they die. Furthermore, these false notions about ourselves carry us to the next life. As long as we remain unconsciously identified with the contents of the mind, these limiting false beliefs about Self will continue to make us miserable in this life and carry us on to the next life for a repeat performance. However, each time you choose to be present with something that is present, like the sound of the Hare Krishna mantra, you come out of the illusory world of the mind and awaken into the reality of life now.

Of course, letting go of identification with the imagined self and acceptance of the true self is what 'surrender' is all about. Surrendering to Krishna is about freeing yourself from limiting beliefs, from your story, from the dream self, from the world of the mind, and assuming your real identity as servant of Krishna. In the dream world of the mind, you imagine that you exist without Krishna. When you are awake in the present, your true self is revealed as existing only because of Krishna. You acknowledge that you exist and that you exist only because God exists. *I belong to Krishna.*

Surrender is a choice and a continuous one at that. What choice do you have? You have free will to choose to live in the reality of life now where God is in control, or you can choose to live in the illusory past / future world of the mind where you imagine that you are in control.

Surrender is a simple choice you make to be awake in the present with whatever is here and present with you because Krishna exists at the centre of everything present. It is a simple choice you can make anytime, anywhere and often. You can choose to be here with the Tulsi plant and thank Krishna for your life. You are either here in the reality of life, or you are not here. It is your choice to be here and no one else's.

The only way you can be *not here* is to go into the mind and become identified with thoughts about past and future. God has given us this slight independence. We have free will to place our attention wherever we choose too. It is up to each one of us to choose the reality of life now or the illusion of life in the mind.

All we have to do is make a conscious choice to be present for Krishna when we chant His Holy Name. Resolve to be present for three mantras at a time. When we are present for Krishna, automatically the illusion of separateness from God dissolves into the light of our awakened consciousness. Without extra effort, we stop imagining that we can enjoy life without God.

Every moment we have this choice - do we choose to live in the reality of life in the present or to be in the illusory mental world of the false self? The false self only exists as thoughts about past and future. That is it. There is nothing wrong with thinking and we need our material identity in order to function in this world. At the same time, an awakened person no longer believes that the world of thought is real or significant. Only consciousness is alive and real.

Consciousness is always now. I challenge you all. Try and not be here! It is impossible.

So, the common misconceptions we have about ourselves such as, *I am not good enough, I am American or Chinese,* etc. form the foundation of the self-image. The self-image or false ego only exists in the world of thought. In the present moment, the imagined self is absent. In the present moment what actually exists is only silent awareness of being.

If I believe that *I am not good enough,* one of the ways to compensate for the fear of not being good enough is to try to be better than everybody else. That manifests as a desire to be special, to be distinct from others, or the *wanting* to be adored by others. Everyone wants to be a movie star, a rock star, or a Kirtan star, or a Guru, which is the ultimate sense gratification. The Wanting to be good enough only exists in thought; not in the now.

In childhood, I learnt to believe that I am not good enough. As a result of this false belief, I now have a compulsion to prove to others that I am unique and special. When I daydream as I chant, this desire to be special in the eyes of others is not only maintained, but magnified. This is my personal example of watering the weeds of material desire that are based on an illusory concept of self while engaged in chanting.

I want to say it again. Forgive me for repeating these words. It is so important to understand. The variety of material desires seem without limit. Where do they come from? All material desires spring up from the same source - ignorance. Ignorance of what? Ignorance of the true self, which becomes our false concept of self, self-image, false ego, etc. The imagined self only exists in the world of thought. The person we imagine ourselves to be does not exist in the present.

Since we don't know who we are and we don't know our real value, we suffer from constant self-doubt. In truth, life is most precious; and valuable for life is the energy of pure consciousness that emanates from Krishna. Life is consciousness. What can be more precious and valuable than the conscious being, Sat-Chit-Ananda?

We are all conscious living beings. But when consciousness is lost in thought, consciousness becomes unconscious and cannot perceive itself. If we are unaware of our life, it means we are not conscious of being conscious. As a result of not being conscious of being conscious, we don't know our real self and our true value. In fact, when we are not awake in the present and conscious of being conscious, we feel less than average. Due to self-doubt, we fearfully and constantly compare ourselves to others. We are afraid of not being good enough or equal to others. From this ignorance of self, the false need to be special takes over our life and also infects our devotional service.

The real cure for the disease of ignorance and the weeds of desire that self-ignorance produces, is true self-discovery. Through the door-way of the present anyone can easily discover the true Self, even right now. Discovery of your true self is not something that is going to occur in the future. It can only happen now. The true self is revealed through the experience of being present. Life only exists right now. The more you choose to live in the present, the more you will experience the sacredness of your life now. Life is a gift from Krishna that He is providing and maintaining without a beginning or end. No one loves us more than Him. He knows who we really are. Maybe we forgot, but Krishna hasn't forgotten.

You love your hands, don't you? Would you want to cut off your hands? Never. All living beings expand from Krishna. Krishna sees us as part of Himself. We are forever intimately related with Krishna. We are part of Him as much as a leaf is part of a tree or sunrays are part of the sun. Our consciousness can never be destroyed or separated from God. When we start to discover that Krishna is the source of our life, then nothing compares to that experience of happiness we feel as we recognize our eternal connection and dependence upon God.

Once we know our true value, we no longer feel afraid. We no longer fear rejection. We don't need other people's approval anymore in order to feel good about ourselves. We stop comparing ourselves with others. We feel whole and complete. We want to serve Krishna out of a feeling of gratitude for the joy we feel moment-to-moment just to be alive. We directly experience the truth of life and our own completeness.

From an inner sense of wholeness, we have pure motive to serve Krishna and we no longer expect anything in return for service to Him. We no longer look outside of ourselves for happiness and satisfaction, because we see Krishna is already giving us everything. I call this, serving Krishna from the sense of fullness that spontaneously arises from the recognition of the completeness of being. This perception of the truth of being is the *weed killer*. Notice your life right now, and say "thank You" to Krishna. By His grace, all is well and taken care of.

Next verse: *prathamei upaśākhāra karaye chedana*

*tabe mūla-śākhā bāḍi' yāya vṛndāvana*

*"As soon as an intelligent devotee sees an unwanted creeper growing beside the original creeper, he must cut it down instantly. Then the real creeper, the bhakti-latā, grows nicely, returns home, back to Godhead, and seeks shelter under the lotus feet of Kṛṣṇa.*

CC Madhya 19.161

Next verse:

*'prema-phala' pāki' paḍe, mālī āsvādayalatā avalambi' mālī 'kalpa-vṛkṣa' pāya*

*"When the fruit of devotional service becomes ripe and falls down, the gardener tastes the fruit and thus takes advantage of the creeper and reaches the desire tree of the lotus feet of Kṛṣṇa in Goloka Vṛndāvana.*

CC Madhya 19.162

Next verse:

*tāhāṅ sei kalpa-vṛkṣera karaye sevana*

**sukhe prema-phala-rasa kare āsvādana**

*"There the devotee serves the lotus feet of the Lord, which are compared to a wish-fulfilling tree. With*

*great bliss he tastes the juice of the fruit of love and becomes eternally happy.*

CC Madhya 19.163

Next verse:

*ṛddhā siddhi-vraja-vijayitā satya-dharmā*
*samādhirbrahmānando gurur api camatkārayaty eva tāvat*
*yāvat premṇāṁ madhu-ripu-vaśī-kāra-siddhauṣadhīnāṁgandho 'py antaḥ-karaṇa-saraṇī-pānthatāṁ na prayāti*

*'As long as there is not the slightest fragrance of pure love of Kṛṣṇa, which is the perfect medicinal herb for controlling Lord Kṛṣṇa within the heart, the opulence of the material perfections known as the siddhis, the Brahminical perfections [satya,* śama, *titikṣā and so on], the trance of the yogīs and the monistic bliss of Brahman all seem wonderful for men.'*

CC Madhya 19.165

The Lord is saying, as long as we don't have the slightest taste for the Holy Name, mystical powers will seem desirable. We may even crave them. However, when a higher taste for the Name has arisen, nothing else other than the Holy Name seems attractive to us.

As we transcend the influence of the mind and senses, taste for chanting will increase. So as long as you don't have that taste for the Holy Name, mystic perfection and the bliss of Brahman all seem attractive. Once we have a taste for the Holy Name, mystical perfection or becoming one with God will lose their glitter.

Does everyone know the definition of pure devotional service?

According to Rupa Goswami: Pure Bhakti is without personal motive, and also without guessing or speculation.

We cannot guess what Krishna wants, or what is pleasing to Him. So, we should avoid the tendency to imagine what is pleasing to Krishna. Instead of guessing, we should ask our Guru how we can please Krishna.

Our Guru has told us that Krishna is pleased when we sincerely chant 16 rounds a day and follow 4 regulative principles for life. Prabhupada has said that we can be certain that our chanting is counted and recorded by Krishna. By innocently following the instruction of our Guru, we can be confident and know that Krishna is pleased by our service.

Since our Gurudev has asked us to chant sixteen rounds a day and follow the regulative principles for life, it is out of love and respect for Guru that we perform this service of daily chanting the Holy Names. If we do this devotional service of daily chanting and avoiding sinful activities, we can know that Krishna is pleased by our service to the Holy Name and Guru. Otherwise, we are guessing or speculating about what pleases Krishna. Krishna accepts service that is performed out of love.

We cannot make it up or do whatever we imagine is pleasing to Krishna, right?

Maybe Krishna and Guru's order is not what I want to do today. I want to sleep a few more hours and only chant 4 rounds and maybe tomorrow I will chant 8 rounds and another day chant 64 laps because that is what I want to do, especially since I have no taste.

But I know without guessing, without doubt, that Guru and Krishna want me to serve them by avoiding sinful actions and chanting at least sixteen rounds on my beads every day. Guru asked and I agreed. Very simple. This much they have asked me to do. Of that, I am certain. So, if I do what pleases Guru and Krishna, that quality of service is devoid of personal desire or speculation. That kind of service allows us entrance into the land of pure Bhakti. I'm not chanting for me; I'm chanting for them, because they are pleased by that chanting. And, I'm not guessing about what will please Krishna.

Lord Caitanya says, we receive the seed of pure Bhakti by serving a pure devotee of Krishna. Devotional service under the guidance of a pure devotee is how a fortunate *Jiva-atma (*individual unit of consciousness*)* becomes situated in pure Bhakti. By following Guru, I am not doing what I want, but rather I am doing what Guru wants. Guru wants what Krishna wants. Serving the Holy Name according to Guru's instruction is what situates us in pure Bhakti, even from the very beginning of chanting. By the mercy of Krishna, one gets a Guru and by the mercy of Guru, one gets Krishna.

The next verse is from Narada Pancharatra, which is the scripture given to us by Narada Muni. Pancha means five, and ratra means nights, so five nights. Narada received this knowledge from Lord Brahma over 5 nights, and Brahma was taught the absolute truth by Krishna in a period of 5 nights, as well. This is because previously, two demons had stolen Brahma's knowledge. Brahma lost his knowledge, so Krishna restored Brahma's knowledge by instructing him for 5 nights. Lord Brahma then passed on this same instruction to his son Narada Muni. This is Guru-parampara. The rules and regulation in deity worship we follow in ISKCON are based on the Narada Pancharatra.

*sarvopādhi-vinirmuktaṁtat-paratvena nirmalam*
*hṛṣīkeṇa hṛṣīkeśa-sevanaṁ bhaktir ucyate*

*'Bhakti, or devotional service, means engaging all our senses in the service of the Lord, the Supreme Personality of Godhead, the master of all the senses. When the spirit soul renders service unto the Supreme, there are two side effects. One is freed from all material designations, and one's senses are purified simply by being employed in the service of the Lord.'*

So here (continue reading CC Madhya 19.170) he's talking about Bhakti, or devotional service. It means we need to engage all our senses in the service of the Lord. The Lord is called Hrishikesha, meaning the Master of senses. When one renders service to the Supreme Lord with the bodily senses there are two results: we become free from material identification with mind and body, and the senses become purified, so we can actually perceive the Lord.

Next verse

*"Just as the celestial waters of the Ganges flow unobstructed into the ocean, so when My devotees*

*simply hear of Me, their minds come to Me. I reside in the hearts of all.*

CC Madhya 19.171

Next verse

*hena kṛṣṇa-nāma yadi laya bahu-bāratabu yadi prema nahe, nahe aśrudhāra tabe jāni, aparādha tāhāte pracurakṛṣṇa-nāma-bīja tāhe nā kare aṅkura*

*If one chants the exalted Holy Name of the Lord again and again, and yet his love for the Supreme Lord does not develop and tears do not appear in his eyes, it is evident that because of his offenses in chanting, the seed of the Holy Name of Kṛṣṇa does not sprout.*

CC Ādi 8.29-30

That is a heavy statement. By the mercy of Krishna and Guru we receive the seed Bhakti and place it in our heart, but if we continue to commit the 10 offenses in chanting, the Bhakti seed doesn't even sprout.

When the Bhakti seed does finally sprout, two small, tender leaves unfold. The first leaf is freedom from all suffering, and the second leaf is auspicious life. We can know that our chanting is effective if our level of suffering in the form of anxiety and lamentation is decreasing and our happiness and inner satisfaction is increasing.

One of the four noble truths of Buddhism is that life is suffering. A famous Greek philosopher said that we do not suffer because of what happens in life. Rather we suffer because of the thoughts we have about what happens in life. When we are identified with the thoughts in our mind, we suffer!

We suffer whenever we lament the past. We may feel all kinds of emotional disturbance as we remember what happened in our life. Perhaps we are still carrying around unresolved anger, sadness, hurt, and fearful feelings about past experiences that occurred ten minutes, ten days or ten years ago or more. We suffer when we imagine the future and worry about what we may lose. We suffer when we hanker after what we imagine will make us happy; and we worry that what we want may never be obtained.

When we are living in the present, there is no lamenting the past or worrying about the future. There is no suffering. On the contrary, we are appreciating our life in the present moment and just being here peacefully chanting the Holy Name.  When we consistently live in the present, we feel peaceful and happy just to be here. The absence of lamentation and hankering and a heart full of gratitude for life as we chant, are solid indications that the seed of Bhakti has sprouted.

According to Rupa Goswami, the initial effect of attentive chanting is klesh-agni or disappearance of suffering. The first leaf that unfolds as the Bhakti plant begins to sprout is freedom from all suffering, Klesha Agni.

Klesha is suffering, Agni is fire. When we have material desires – we are here but we want to be there – our mind is craving something we don't have or wanting to get away from something we do have. This mental wanting and not wanting, iccha-dvesha, is the essence of suffering. We are identified with thoughts and lost in the illusory world of the mind seeking to get something or get rid of something. We feel disconnected, dissatisfied and incomplete. The unconscious mental pattern of chasing after pleasure and running away from pain causes consciousness to remain trapped and bewildered, spinning round and round in the mind and then catapulted into the next life. Samsara dava......

## SP-Letter to Susan Beckman -- Herts, England August 29, 1973:

*The chanting is a process of purification. Just like we use soap to cleanse the body - this is material, but chanting is spiritual cleansing. The three stages of cleansing are first to clean the mirror of the mind. In the Bhagavad Gita it is said, "The mind is the best friend and the worst enemy, for one who has learned to control the mind it is the best of friends but for one who has failed to do so, it is the worst enemy." Due to long-term association, the mind absorbed in material things has become contaminated, or dirty; the chanting process purifies such a mind. Then the next stage, when the mind is cleansed, one becomes free from the symptoms of material existence. Material existence means to be always hankering and lamenting. I must have a new automobile, I must have more money, I must have good wife, I must have this, I must have that. Then when I have the thing, I lament, I have lost my wife, I have lost my money, I have lost my car, simply lamenting. So, the second stage is to be free from this anxiety. The third stage is, "He never laments nor desires to have anything; he is equally disposed to every living entity. In that state he attains pure devotional service unto me." Bhagavad Gita 18.54*

The cause of suffering is described by Srila Visvanatha Chakravarti Thakura in his Madhurya Kadambini. Actually, he is quoting from Patanjali's Yoga-sutra. Patanjali also talks about the root of suffering and how it manifests. There are five aspects of suffering.

The first is ignorance; we forget who we are. In truth, we are eternally conscious and connected to Krishna. Ignorance of our true self and our eternal connection with the absolute truth is the root of suffering.

From ignorance arises the false conception of self, called Ahankara.

Prabhupada writes in BG 13.8-12, purport:

*False ego means accepting this body as oneself. When one understands that he is not his body and is a spirit soul, he comes to his real ego. Ego is there. False ego is condemned, but not real ego. In the Vedic literature (Brihad-aranyaka Upanishad 1.4.10) it is said, aham brahmasmi: I am Brahman, I am spirit. This "I am," the sense of self, also exists in the liberated stage of self-realization. This sense of "I am" is ego, but when the sense of "I am" is applied to this false body it is false ego.*

So, it is due to ignorance and the false ego that we do not feel connected to our true self and to the source of life, Sri Krishna. Instead, we feel disconnected and dissatisfied. When consciousness is identified with thought, we are in a certain state of unconsciousness or ignorance and cannot perceive our real self as the witnessing presence of consciousness.

Out of ignorance arises the false sense of self that feels disconnected and incomplete from the source of life. The false self is inherently afraid and in a fight for survival. The false ego craves pleasure and resists pain in the never-ending struggle to exist and prevent death. From the false ego, arises material desire and hate, *"I want this and I don't want that."* From ignorance arises the fear of impermanence and death. Fear of dying is always at the back of our mind, right?

No matter what we are doing, the fear that it may all suddenly end exists at the back of our mind. The fear of death has a synergistic effect on material desires for happiness in this world. Two substances separately may not appear to be very strong. However, when the two substances are combined together, they support each other and become stronger. That is called synergy. So, the fear of death actually may increase material attachments. *"I better do this or get that before I die. Time is running out."*

If we are chanting and committing offenses, we will still feel unhappy and suffer, because our consciousness continues to be entangled and identified with the thoughts in the mind.

Under the influence of ignorance, consciousness believes that the thoughts in the mind are real and significant. Due to ignorance, consciousness identifies with thoughts about the past and future. As a result, we do not perceive our true being of consciousness which exists in the eternal now.

We suffer because we still cling to the belief in a false concept of our self. When a person is lost in the mind and identifying with the false self, there will be hankering for happiness in the future and lamenting about what happened in the past. As long as one is not awake in the present, one will not be present for the Holy Name. Suffering and the fear of death will persist until one awakens in the present and chooses to be present for the Holy Name.

If you consciously choose to live in the truth of life that is revealed to you in the present, all of the five causes of suffering disappear; because, when you are consciously present, you come out of the mind and begin to directly experience your true being.

The mind's business is to think, and thinking is always about past or future. But you are just here when you choose to be present with something that is present with you, like *Tulsidevi*. When consciousness is present, thoughts stop without you even trying to stop them. When you are awake in the present, the mind is silent and you are perfectly aware of being. By choosing to live in the present, without extra effort, you can begin to perceive your true self and your personal connection with the Lord. In the awakened state of consciousness called presence, you can be present for Krishna in the form of His Holy Name and chant peacefully without material expectations. Your practice is to simply chant and disregard memory and expectations for at least three mantras.

But as long as you continue to chant inattentively, which is an offense, Lord Caitanya says that even though you may have received the seed of Bhakti, the seed does not sprout. So, one way you can determine where you are on the path of Bhakti is to notice if you are truly happy within or not. If you don't feel the joy of being in this moment, it means you are lost in the mind and not present for Krishna when you chant. The seed of devotion has sprouted in a person who is steadily happy within, and no longer laments the past or craves happiness in the future.

We were having a discussion in Lanzhou. We were talking about the 10 offenses: there's a purport in Caitanyacaritāmṛta where Prabhupada defines the ten offenses in chanting with a slightly different definition as compared to the definition stated in the Krishna Consciousness song book. The song book's list of the ten offenses which is based upon the version translated from the Padma-purana. (Everyone started listing the definitions of 10 offenses)

It's really important that we know what the ten offenses to the Holy Name are, and understand them so we can avoid them.

The first offense, offending Vaishnavas, is potentially a problem for all of us. Actually, Visvanatha Chakravarti Thakura says, offending any living entity is offensive and detrimental to pure chanting of the Holy Name.

Who is a Vaishnava? The Nectar of Instruction talks about three types of Vaishnavas - the novice, intermediate and advanced devotee. Once Lord Caitanya was asked, who is a Vaishnava? Actually, He was asked this same question three years in a row by the same person and each time the Lord gave a slightly different answer. Mahaprabhu says that anyone who chants the Hare Krishna Mantra, even once, can be considered to be a Vaishnava.

The best defence is a good offense. Therefore, we should proactively offer respects to everyone. For anyone who is chanting, we should at least mentally respect them and appreciate them because they have faith in the Holy Name. In spite of whatever personality flaws a Vaishnava might have, to their credit they have faith in the Holy Name and we must be careful to acknowledge how auspicious it is for anyone to be chanting. We should know that to chant the Holy Name, especially with faith, is not a common thing. It's very rare. Let us all be careful to mentally offer our respects to whoever is chanting the Holy Names. Be especially cautious to not offend, blame, or unnecessarily criticize anyone chanting the Holy Names.

A Vaishnava who is initiated, chanting sixteen rounds and trying to avoid the ten offenses in chanting, is considered to be a very serious and committed Vaishnava. Everyone here in this room today is very a committed Vaishnava. You are all sincerely giving your life to this chanting. Chanting of the Holy Names is an eternal spiritual activity. The results of chanting can never be lost or diminished in any way. Our material personality, with all its defects, is going to suddenly disappear one day. Knowing this fact, let us choose to be liberal and accepting towards each other. We should be very accepting of others' faults, because our temporary material identity is illusory and not really a big deal in the view of eternity. Let us all recognize what is of real significance, which is that we are on this path back to Godhead, chanting the Holy Name. Chanting God's name is a spiritual activity that descends from the spiritual sky. Towards a Vaishnava, who is initiated and seriously chanting, we should bow down our head to the floor and pay our respects, as long as you are not in public, of course.

For the advanced devotees who have been steadily chanting for many years, who are peaceful and setting a sublime example for others to follow by their behaviour of friendly equanimity, who particularly exhibit no urge to criticize others, toward such an advanced Vaishnava, we should be eager to serve and hear from them.

Being enthusiastic to respect all Vaishnavas is being proactive. We want to be careful and avoid offenses to all living beings, especially Vaishnavas of all kinds. We can best guard against committing the first offense by proactively looking for the good in each other. Be like a honey bee and go after the honey. Try to serve each other. Then, we are much less likely to offend Vaishnavas in the first place.

However, inevitably in the course of daily life, we sometimes, intentionally or not, do hurt and offend Vaishnavas. In the day-to-day interaction with others, if we neglect or hurt another person, what are we to do? We are bound to neglect each other or become irritated by each other from time to time. Familiarity breeds contempt.

As soon as we recognize our mistake, we should admit it. Without delay, it is best to go up to the person who we have offended, confess our mistake, and ask to be forgiven.

We can say, *I am sorry*. Admit the mistake and say, *'Please forgive me'.*

Talking to each other face-to-face, taking responsibility with and honest confession, and asking forgiveness are vitally important for healthy relationships, both materially and spiritually; because, when we offend each other, our hearts close, and the way the closed heart manifests is, *"I don't want to be with that person"*. When the heart is closed, it's painful. If you are around someone who you hold a grudge against, your heart is closed and it's painful to be around a person against whom your heart has closed. So, you want to get away. So then, how can you chant with love and gratitude when your heart is closed? You cannot.

Spiritual life is about self-improvement and taking responsibility for the results of your actions. This means you must accept responsibility for the consequences of your thoughts, words and actions. Make a confession. Say you are sorry. Ask for forgiveness. These are the steps necessary to reopen the heart and to keep the heart open. Honestly admitting the fact when you have offended a Vaishnava and asking for forgiveness is the only remedy for Vaishnava aparadha.

On the other hand, what if someone has hurt or offended you? If this happens to you and your heart closes towards a Vaishnava, then what to do? First admit to yourself how you feel. Then consciously allow yourself to feel the feeling of anger, hurt and sadness. Feelings come from thoughts and thoughts come from our own egos. Assuming responsibility for the condition of your own mind does not excuse the misbehaviour of someone else. You are simply taking responsibility for the response of your own mind. Remember the Avanti Brahman.

## SB 11.23.42

*The brahmana said: These people are not the cause of my happiness and distress. Neither are the demigods, my own body, the planets, my past work, or time. Rather, it is the mind alone that causes happiness and distress and perpetuates the rotation of material life.*

As soon as possible, notice the tightness around your heart area and take responsibility by owning the feeling. You can consciously feel the pain of a closed heart. By admitting that the painful feeling is your creation, you realize you are not a victim. Admit that the pain you feel inside is “your” pain. The admission of your mind-identified state of consciousness is a necessary step to take if you are to arise in mastery of your own mind and ego.

Next, confess how you feel to the Lord of the heart. *Oh, Lord, just see, I feel angry. I feel hurt. I want revenge, etc.* After you have noticed, felt and confessed how you feel to the Lord, relax and let the memory go, just for now. Admit to the Lord that the reason you are hurting is because you have again fell into ignorance and forgotten your true self and the Lord. Feel compassion for your own susceptibility to ignorance. Having compassion towards your own self will allow you to feel compassion towards the one who harmed you.

It is very purifying to confess to the Lord and to admit your mistakes. Confessing to the Lord beforehand can also help you prepare for making an honest confession to the devotee from whom you need to apologize and ask to be forgiven.

After confessing to the Lord, you can approach the devotee you offended and ask to be forgiven. It’s the Lord’s and the devotee’s forgiveness that you need.

Even if the devotee or person you hurt is no longer physically near you or alive, you can still confess and ask for forgiveness from the core of your being to the Lord of the heart.

Bottom line, a devotee is careful not to offend any living entity. However, if we do hurt another living being, we should be quick to make amends. Holding ill will towards another living being contaminates our consciousness and closes the door of our heart. Prabhupada writes that *we should not become a source of dread to anyone.* We can resolve not to become a source of dread by thoughts, words or actions. Let us make a conscious effort to avoid mental and verbal criticism, or reactively blaming others. Resist the temptation to harm anyone. Anger, criticism and blame are symptoms of a closed heart.

We need an open heart if we are to have a functional relationship with anyone, including our relationship with the Lord. The chanting of His Holy Name is performed with an open heart that is free from malice. If you close your heart to any living being, you close your heart to the Lord of the heart who is exists at the centre of everything and everyone. It is a mistake to think that devotees exist separate from the Lord or in some other location. Devotees and the Lord are not separate. The vision of a materialistic devotee is one of separation which is created by the duality of delusion. The materialistic devotee's consciousness is absorbed in identification with the past / future world of the mind. Please see BG 7.27.

The misconception of separation of life from the Lord of life is a major obstacle to reaching the stage of steadiness in Bhakti. The more we are caught in the mind's chatter, the more we feel separate from the reality of life revealed through the gateway of the present. We feel separate from the present reality and from each other. We feel separate from the source of life, and God.

In fact, if we closely observe human motivation, human action is always an attempt to resolve or escape from the feeling of separation, the loneliness that exists at the deepest level of our unconscious being. But as you awaken to the reality of life in the present, which never goes away and is always available to you, you can chant peacefully and steadily no matter what is occurring in the external environment. As you awaken in the present reality, you no longer feel separate from yourself or God. You always feel connected with the truth of life. The illusion of separation has dissolved into the light of the present.

The novice devotee, commonly called the third-level devotee, does not yet realize a conscious connection to the Lord. The third-level devotee is lost in identification with the mind and has yet to experience the truth of life and how everyone and everything in existence is connected to the Lord. We should not remain on this third level of consciousness. Prabhupada says, as soon as possible one should come to the second level devotee position. From the second level devotee position one is better able to distinguish who is a devotee, and avoid offending Vaishnavas and other living beings.

Now the second offense may not appear as relevant to people who are not born in India or raised in the Hindu culture. Most westerners are unfamiliar with Demi-gods.

The second offense states that it is an offense to the Holy Name if you consider the Demi-gods to be equal to or the same as Lord Vishnu. But there is another aspect to the second offense we must consider as well.

The way the second offense reads in the song book is that, one should not consider the names of Demi-gods and the names of the Lord to be equal or the same. But there is another aspect of this offense mentioned in other writings of the Acharya's and which is not well known. Prabhupada and Bhaktivinod Thakur have said that it is also an offense to consider the Lord, who is an individual sentient person, and the Lord's name to be separate and different from each other. In other words, if we imagine that the Lord as a person is different or separate from His name, or is not personally present in His name, that is an offense, as well.

We are also eternal persons, but our materially designated names and our true self are not one & the same. Basically, as long as we are influenced by the mode of ignorance, which is the state of consciousness being identified with the mind, our consciousness is under the delusion of duality. Everything we perceive through the mind's lens of duality, appears to be separated. We see ourself and everyone and everything as separate from each other and separate from the Lord. As long as we are not awake in the present and believe in our thoughts and live in the illusory world of the mind, we can't help but commit the offense of imagining that the form of the Lord and His Holy Name are separate and different. We hear the Name but don't perceive the Lord's form. Due to ignorance, we will consider the Name of the Lord and the Lord Himself to be different from each other, and this is an offense. We imagine that although the sound of the name of the Lord is here, the Lord Himself is somewhere else and not present here. We ignore the presence of the Lord in the form of His name and don't even know we are ignoring Him.

We commit this offense (of considering the Lord different from His name) when we are not present for the Holy Name. We then treat the Holy Name as if the Lord is not present with us in the form of His name by ignoring Him. If we are not present for Krishna in the form of his name, it is because we cannot recognize that the form of the Lord and the Lord's name are actually present before us as holy sound vibration. Due to absorption in our thoughts, we cannot perceive that the Holy Name and the form of the Lord are one & the same, and not separate from each other. We imagine the sound of the Name is here, and the Lord's form is somewhere else. GoLoka (Supreme abode of Lord Krsna with his cows in spiritual world) is somewhere over there and not here. If we are under the misconception that the Lord and His name are separate, that is offensive. Considering the Lord to be different from His Holy Name, is also an aspect of the second offense in chanting.

The third offense in chanting is to disobey the order of the spiritual master or to consider Gurudev to be an ordinary man. If you have personal association with the spiritual master, there is the dangerous possibility of becoming too familiar and committing the third offense. This is another example of how familiarity can breed contempt. Under these circumstances you might start to think that Gurudev is a common person.

The person Guru and Guru's instruction are also one and not separate. To disobey or neglect guru's instruction is an offense to the Holy Name. After all, the Holy Name has come to us through our Gurudev. In any case, if you neglect Gurudev's order to chant 16 rounds and follow 4 regulative principles, this will be a serious hinderance to the awakening of pure Krishna Bhakti and chanting *suddhanama.*

The spiritual master also has to be cautious in his interactions with his disciples. Gurudev must avoid putting the student in a situation where the student becomes unable to follow his order.

One day I had a personal conversation with Srila Prabhupada after he had eaten lunch prasadam.

Prabhupada asked me to share Krishna's teachings in Japan. He, "asked me" as opposed to ordering me. He had actually made the same request on two previous occasions under different circumstances. Interestingly, Prabhupada framed his request as a question; thus, making it a choice. He gave me a choice, not an order. *Would you be willing to stay in Japan and teach about*

*Krishna?* Prabhupada often presented his order in such a way that the disciple would have a choice to say yes or no. The Guru can make a humble request to his disciple. If, for some reason, the disciple cannot agree to it, then his refusal does not become an offense.

I remember the last time Prabhupada visited Japan, he asked me to stay in Japan. Prabhupada said, "I would like you to stay in Japan and preach; are you willing to do that?" I said yes, I would. So, he gave me the option.

There are also times when the Guru's instruction is not negotiable. For example, at the time of initiation, the Guru requests the student to chant sixteen rounds, avoid the ten offenses in chanting and following the four regulative principles for life. Prior to initiation one voluntarily chooses to accept Guru's instructions and follow them. After receiving initiation, one must keep the promise for life.

The instruction of the Guru to chant sixteen rounds a day and follow the four regulative principles is our main service to Guru and Krishna. This instruction of Gurudev is not arbitrary. If we somehow come to neglect the Guru's instruction in this matter, that is an offense to the Holy Name.

It's not the Guru's duty to micromanage a disciple's life, like *"you should get married, you should have 10 children,"* etc. You should not bring those kinds of personal questions to your Guru either. Sometimes Prabhupada would say, *"The Lord is in your heart, ask Him."* In all seriousness Prabhupada would often encourage his disciples to ask the Lord within for answers.

It is worthy to note that Vyasadeva did not approach his Guru, Narada Muni, with questions until Vyasa had first exhaustively introspected within himself for the answer as to why he was feeling dissatisfied after having written all the Vedas.

Now the fourth offense: again, this may not be as much of an issue for those who are from non-Hindu cultures. It is an offense to the Holy Name to criticize Vedic literature and other sacred literature that contain similar conclusion regarding the Absolute Truth. Followers of Lord Caitanya are non-sectarian and appreciate God wherever God is found. The Bible also states that the name of God is holy.

The fifth offense is to believe that the glories of the Holy Name are exaggerations or imagination. Ok, let me ask you: scripture says if you chant the Holy Name of the Lord even once, or even unconsciously, you are immediately freed of all sinful reactions. Do you believe that? (Everyone says yes) Are you sure? Why not, right? But if you doubt that, or if you hear such glorifications of the Holy Name and you think, "Hmmm, I don't think so...", then you might be making an offense. But I think for most of you on the path of Krishna Consciousness, that's not the case, right?

Offense number six is to make up your own meaning of the Holy Name. I think most of you are not making your own interpretations about the meaning of the Holy Name either. Is this a fair statement?

Offense number seven: I don't think most of you are committing sins on the strength of chanting, either. Are you? That doesn't mean that you and I sometimes don't unintentionally commit sins; we all commit sins. It is offensive if a person chants with the mentality, *I'm chanting Hare Krishna, so I think I will go have a hamburger and because I am chanting, there will be no karma for killing and eating an animal.* I think it is safe to say that none of you present here today are intentionally committing sins and then expecting that because you are chanting there will be no sinful reaction to pay. To commit sins on the strength of chanting is to actually have an intention: *I will nullify reactions from sins by chanting and go on committing sins.*

The eighth offense in chanting is to believe that chanting is in the same category as just another religious ritual to be performed. I don't think you all believe chanting is just another way to get blessings, or a ritual to obtain religious merit in order to go to the heavenly planets.

Offense number nine: It is an offense to the Holy Name to preach the glories of the Holy Name to the faithless. There are some fanatic devotees pushing Krishna Consciousness onto others whether the people they are preaching to are interested or not. Being overzealous for converting others to Krishna Consciousness is really a sign of immaturity and ultimately can be counterproductive. Fanatical preaching often arises out of a herd mentality that is associated with groups of individuals on lower levels of consciousness.

Why is such forceful preaching about the Holy Name to faithless people an offense? That's because, attempting to convince people who are not interested in chanting the Holy Name and do not want to hear what you have to say, is damaging to the person that you are trying to persuade. If members of the public, or friends or family are not interested in listening to your preaching, it is better for you and for them to be left alone. It is especially harmful when you force uninterested people to listen to you even after they have told you that they are not interested in what you have to say. The result is that such people will grow to dislike Krishna and not respect His devotees. The effects of preaching to the faithless is bad for them and for you; because, Bhakti is about love. Love requires free will. Free will requires a choice. Love cannot be forced. Love for Krishna cannot be forced.

Sharing the glories of the Holy Name to the uninformed, requires the devotee to have great integrity.

## Integrity defined:

- The quality of being honest and having strong moral principles; moral uprightness.
- The state of being whole and undivided.

Srila Bhaktisiddhanta taught his disciples: ***Do not hear*** *from the mouths of persons lacking proper conduct. If your conduct is below par, you should not publicly preach about the Lord. Close the door and preach to yourself. Bhajan really begins when one's outside and inside are the same."*

So, one way we can avoid committing the ninth offense is by remembering what is called the Ripe Mango Principle. I first heard the Ripe Mango principle from

Vaisesika Prabhu. He's an expert preacher and book distributor. Vaisesika Prabhu teaches,

*Don't pick the mango from the tree until it's ripe.*

What happens when you pick a green mango? It stays green and it will never ripen. So, if we are preaching to people who are not open and not interested to hear about the glories of the Holy Name, we are actually hurting their chances of becoming Krishna Conscious, now and in the future. This kind of so-called preaching is really egocentric enthusiasm. It is fanaticism, which is damaging and is a form of violence.

We will discuss the tenth offense in chanting soon.

But first, I want to read aloud the ten offenses as Prabhupada has defined them in this purport of Caitanyacaritāmṛta. His words are illuminating and pure nectar. I want to compare Prabhupada's definition of the ten offenses with the song books translations of the ten offenses.

Let us read once more the ten offenses in chanting as they are stated in the Vaishnavas' song book that is originally translated from Sanskrit verses of the Padma-parana.

(Everyone together read the 10 offenses in the song book)

Okay let's read together and contemplate the meaning of the ten offenses as stated in the song book. Again, we are reading the translation of the ten offenses from the Sanskrit version in the Padma-purana that most devotees are familiar with, and are recited daily around the world of ISKCON.

Now read aloud the tenth offense to the Holy Name as stated in the song book.

Okay, now let us focus on the tenth offense in chanting. The song book states that the tenth offense is to maintain material attachments even after understanding so many instructions on this matter and also to be inattentive while chanting. Let us discuss the tenth offense in chanting in more nuanced detail.

What does it mean to maintain material attachment? I bet, each one of you has various and differing ideas concerning the definition of what material attachment means to you. What is your definition of material attachment? To maintain material attachment is a concept that can cover pretty broad area and seems quite abstract. How are we going to understand the notion of maintaining material attachment and apply this understanding to our life and chanting?

When you read the words *to maintain material attachment*, what does this mean to you? Right now, I want you to seriously think about this topic. You can even take a moment to write down your thoughts on this matter. What comes up in your mind? Define material attachment to yourself. Practically speaking, what does it mean to maintain material attachment in your life? What kinds of material attachments are you maintaining? If we are to avoid this offense, then I think it is very important to clarify and understand specifically what is meant by the phrase, *to maintain material attachments*.

*Sanga devotees started to answer this question. To give some examples of the answers they gave -- people are attached to big houses, women love buying beautiful clothes, people have attachment to money, craving name and fame and being emotionally attached to family members.*

Guru replies to the last one: I don't know about you, but I'm pretty emotionally attached to my family members, especially my grandsons. I worship my grandsons more than my deities. I'm pretty emotionally attached to all of you, too.

*Another devotee answers: Desiring to enjoy this material world.*

Guru replies: That's pretty concrete, but also a little broad, too general. Say something more specific.

*Another devotee says: I think it's the enjoyment we derive from our eyes, ears, nose, etc.*

Guru replies: Wanting sensual experiences. I think devotees have more sensual experiences than most people. We enjoy the smell of flowers, seeing beautiful pictures, hearing sublime sounds of music and dance.

I don't know about you, but for a long time my conception of material attachment was being attached to physical things like women, cars, a nice place to live, nice clothes, and family.

I also believed that a sign of spiritual advancement was to give up family and wear saffron-coloured clothes. But one could argue that these examples of material attachment are external and don't describe the root cause of material attachment. As a new devotee, I was taught to believe that material attachment meant being attached to the opposite sex. This may be true, but is there a root cause to being attached to sex life?

When I lived in the temple, there was a routine that would be followed. The same routine is still going on in most temples; after Mangal-artik there's Tulsipuja, everyone sits down and recites Lord Caitanya's

Siksastakam and the list of the ten offenses in chanting. As I recited the ten offenses aloud every morning, I had a certain concept in mind about the phrase, *to maintain material attachment*. I am sure when you repeat the tenth offense in chanting, some image or concept of what material attachment is goes through your mind, as well. As a Brahmachari, I was told never to look at or talk to women. I thought that I was not committing the tenth offense in chanting if I just avoided the opposite sex.

What does the phrase, *to maintain material attachment*, actually mean to you? This is what I'm trying to get at here. Why is it important to examine the meaning of this phrase?

Like you all said, to be attached to enjoying the material world, being attached to this body, these may be examples of material attachments. It is all true. But there is a deeper and more profound material attachment that has captured our consciousness. What is at the root of all material attachment? We have to clearly understand what the root of material attachment is, if we are going to be able to let go of maintaining material attachment and chant *suddha-nama.*

In my humble opinion, the definition given in the Vaishnavas song book of material attachment is very general and it may be helpful for us to investigate the concept of material attachment further. In our Vaishnava literature is there a concise definition of material attachment that captures and defines the essence of material attachment. What essentially does it mean to maintain material attachment?

What is material attachment and how do we maintain it?

The words, material attachment, are vague and nonspecific. Every devotee has their own ideas about what material attachment means to them, personally.

Now let's listen to Prabhupada's definition of material attachment as written in the Caitanya Caritamrita, Adi lila Chapter 8 verse 24 purports:

*If one has heard the glories of the transcendental Holy Name of the Lord but nevertheless continues in a materialistic concept of life, thinking "I am this body and everything belonging to this body is mine [ahaṁ mameti]," and does not show respect and love for the chanting of the Hare Kṛṣṇa mahā-mantra, that is an offense.*

Amazing! All glories to Prabhupada! Prabhupada's definition of material attachment and how material attachments are maintained are very specific, concise and profound.

Material attachment is to mistakenly consider the material mind and body as oneself. *I am this body and I am these thoughts and everything in relationship to this body is mine.*

The root cause of material attachment is lack of true self-awareness, which is a form of ignorance. Ignoring the truth about yourself and your connection with God is how the living being maintains a false sense of identity. Material attachment arises out of ignorance of our true being as pure consciousness that emanates from the source of life, Sri Krishna. As a result of the mind-identified state of consciousness, we feel incomplete and we imagine that we exist separate from the source of life, Sri Krishna. Material desires arise out of a feeling of dissatisfaction that arises from the illusory mind identified state of consciousness.

Whenever we are thinking and don't know we are thinking, we are in ignorance and can no longer perceive our true self. When we are identified with thought, we lose consciousness. We are no longer conscious about the fact that we are conscious. The screen of our mind is full of internal pictures. These internal pictures act as a curtain to prevent the mind from reflecting the true image of our self as the pure light of consciousness.

Prabhupada explains that we maintain material attachment whenever our consciousness is identified with material thoughts and we are believing the false narrative going on in our mind: *I am this mind and body and that everything in relationship to this body is mine.*

To maintain material attachment means to hold on to this false idea of one's self, *I am this body. Everything belongs to me and I exist independent of God.* The materialistic concept of life, *I am this body and everything belongs to me,* is the essence of our self-image. The self-image only exists in the mind space as thoughts, memories and imaginings of the future. The self-image disappears in the present moment when we become self-aware and conscious of being conscious.

In the mind there is an image of the body and things in relationship to the body; a series of pictures, a mentally-constructed self with a story. We maintain this false concept of ourselves whenever we are unconsciously identified with thoughts in the mind. Our mental computer is running in default mode. When we are not awake in the present, we become unconscious of our true self as a being of pure consciousness, the one who consciously knows the thoughts. Our addiction to thinking maintains the false conception of ourselves and all material attachment that flows from the false conception of ourselves.

When our consciousness is lost in thoughts daydreaming, the false conception of our self, *I exist separate from Krishna*, causes us to feel incomplete and dissatisfied. Ignorance of our true self is the reason we crave material enjoyment in all its unlimited varieties. We imagine ourselves as separate from the source of life. As a result, we feel disconnected from our true self and our source. Therefore, we feel incomplete and dissatisfied within. The inner pain of dissatisfaction causes us to search outside of ourself for happiness, and develop so many material attachments.

Our mind is distracted by thoughts and cannot be still for even one moment. It is the Kali-yuga, and we are victims of the monkey mind. The restless and dissatisfied mind is voraciously wondering, *what is next?* We are continually on a search for the next new gadget, next companion, next change of location and next method to enlightenment. We are mentally addicted to the never-ending anticipation of finding fulfilment in the future.

The promise of future fulfilment is one of the false ego's most effective deceptions to keep consciousness lost in the mind and prevent consciousness from the possibility of awakening in the present moment. The ultimate attainment for the false ego is future enlightenment. On the quest for happiness and liberation, the ego/ mind is always eager to try out each new teaching and teacher it comes in contact with. The anticipation of the **new next / next new** keeps the false ego's hope alive and also keeps conscious unaware of itself and lost in thought. As long as we seek what we already are - which is eternal consciousness - we will never stop in the present long enough to realize the truth of who we really are.

How do we maintain a false conception of self? Just by constant thinking, we feed the imagined self with our undivided attention. The false conception of who we are exists in the world of thought. Who we imagine ourselves to be, is no more than mental pictures projected on the screen of the mind. When consciousness is absorbed in and identified with thought, unconsciously thinking, we maintain the illusory idea of ourself as a separate material being.

We maintain our false self-image by continuous and unconscious thinking. When we daydream, we are maintaining and energizing this false sense of who we are. When we are unconsciously thinking about the past and the future, we are reinforcing and maintaining the false notion that *I am* this body and mind and that *I exist independent of God*. If we are lost in daydreaming while we are chanting, then we are especially reinforcing the illusion that *I am this mind and body*.

When we chant and at the same time day-dream, the energy of consciousness is concentrated and absorbed into the false sense of self that is being reflected upon the screen of the mind. The mental image of who we are, is like a sponge soaking up the water of consciousness. When we are chanting and at the same time distracted by thoughts, we are not present and lost in thoughts. Even worse, as we chant inattentively, we are meditating on and strengthening our specific material attachment. Then we are surprised at our lack of spiritual progress!

Distracted chanting is a serious obstacle to awakening. When we are not present for the Holy Name, just the opposite of what we want is occurring. We solidify and sustain the false concept we have of ourselves and maintain material attachments. This is an offense. We are ignoring the Lord. We are actually watering the weeds of material desire that grow in the soil of the misconception we have of ourselves.

If you know the secret of awakening, which is to use your free will intelligently and choose to live in the present, you will awaken out of the dream-world of the mind. When you are present, the false concept of yourself disappears, at least for the moments you are present. Even a few moments awake in the present are very significant. Most people spend lifetimes dreaming and never even awaken for a few seconds.

When you are conscious of being conscious in the present, you are no longer maintaining your false sense of self. The more you are awake in the present, the more you awaken out of the dream state of forgetfulness of your true self and your relationship with the source of life, Sri Krishna. When you bring your attention to the reality of life in the present by noticing whatever is present with you, the mind falls silent. Thoughts stop without you trying to stop them. When you are present, there are no material desires, because material desires only exist in the mind as thoughts about past and future. Be present, chant and be happy.

For the moments you are present, you are an awakened being. The more you choose to be present, the more you awaken and the more your true self is revealed. When you are awake in the present, there is just conscious awareness of being and awareness of whatever is here in the environment with you. Be conscious that you are conscious as you chant and hear the Holy Name.

Who is here? Silent knowing, *I am*. Who is chanting? *I am*. Who is hearing the Holy Name? *I am*. Only you can choose to be present for Krishna in the form of His Holy Name. It is your choice and no one else's. Choosing to live in the reality of the present and leave the illusory world of the mind is the proper use of free will. Resolve to be conscious of being conscious for three mantras at a time. No doubt, you will awaken, but don't take my word for it. You must verify it for yourself.

I am not saying that you need to be present twenty-four hours a day. Just be present for three mantras, over and over. If you can spend a few minutes a day awake in the reality of the present, it will open you up to a heightened awareness of the divinity of life. This heightened awareness will, in turn, transform you. You will begin to experience the truth of who you are as a divine being - i.e., part and parcel of God. You always have been a divine spark of the Supreme and you will always be an expression of the Divine.

The present moment is the gateway to awaken out of the dream world of the mind and into the reality of life in the present. When you consciously choose to live in the present, without extra effort, you start to perceive your true being. When you are present, automatically you come out of the mind and out of the misconception you have of yourself, at least for the moments you are awake in the present. Presence is the foundation for spiritual awakening and for Bhakti — love for self, love others and love for the Lord.

Being self-aware in the present is just a simple choice you make to bring your conscious attention to the present moment. As a human being, you have the power and gift of self-awareness. You can place conscious attention anywhere you want and anytime you want. You can choose to be here, present, or you can choose not to be here. To not be here, you have to go into your mind and think about past and future. It is just a simple choice to be here in the reality of life or go into the illusory world of material thought. Thoughts contain no reality or life. Thoughts are no more than internal pictures being reflected on the movie screen of the mind.

When you choose to be present with something that is present with you, (like for e.g., the Tulsi tree) and the sound of the Holy Name, thoughts stop without you trying to stop them. The world of the false self exists only in the world of thought. As soon as you are present, you transcend the world of thought and the false conception of self. You come out of the illusion of separation from God. You feel connected to your source, the source of life. Then you feel satisfied within.

By direct experience, you sense that your life comes from a greater life, Krishna. Then you feel very satisfied because you no longer view anything as separate from Krishna. You know that nothing exists without Krishna. Your house, your car, your family members, your grandchildren - you see it all in relationship to Krishna. You can only have this vision of the truth of life when you are self-aware in the present moment. Material attachments dissolve in the light of your awakened consciousness. In this moment, do you have any problems?

I am not saying that being awake in the present is a permanent state of consciousness. In truth, there is only life in this moment. Thoughts and sensations constantly change, coming and going. Nothing but the background of awareness is constant and unchanging;

but you can only know this truth from the present. Once you know where the truth is, which is in the present, you are free to choose presence. You can consistently choose to be awake in the truth of your being that is perceivable in the present, especially when you chant the Holy Name.

In fact, as you shift your consciousness to live more fully in the present, the qualities of who you really are, automatically flow into your day-to-day life and relationships. When you are present, you are naturally loving and accepting of yourself and others. There is no excessive judgment or criticism because you view yourself and others as they are now, as opposed to how you viewed them in the past. You have more affection for friends and family.

Affection for friends and family is not a problem because your affection is not based on an illusion. Rather, your love arises spontaneously from the perception of the supreme reality that we are all part of Krishna. Everything that exists can only exist because of Krishna.

So, we have to scan within to examine our thoughts, and notice when we are perpetuating the false concept of ourselves. *Am I living in the reality of the world of here and now? Or am I lost in the mind and daydreaming about past and future? Am I living in the reality of here or the illusion of not here? Observe your mind and come back to the reality of life now. Repeat, repeat, repeat and smile without judging yourself.*

Allow yourself to become acutely aware of any judgmental, critical thoughts you are having toward yourself and others whenever such thoughts arise in mind. Judgmental thoughts are almost always based on illusory beliefs we have about ourselves and others. Just notice the judgmental thinking without judgment and return to present moment awareness. Honestly acknowledge you are having judgmental thoughts and admit it to the Super-soul. *Oh, there is judgmental thinking going on inside my head. Did you see that Lord?* When you become conscious of thought, even judgmental thought, thoughts can no longer exert control over you.

You always have a choice. Which world do you choose to live in? You can choose the illusory past / future world of the mind or the reality of life in the present. Which world do you choose? We are all eternal beings with the gift of free will. You always have a choice to live in the truth of life experienced in the present or the illusion of life created when consciousness is absorbed in thinking. The choice is yours. Only you can decide. Free will is God's gift to you and even Krishna will not interfere with how you use this awesome power, i.e., the power to choose where you place your attention.

When you are daydreaming, you are unconsciously thinking. Your consciousness is identified with thought. You are unconscious of being alive. Your consciousness is lost in the illusory world of the mind. It is by unconscious thinking that we maintain a false concept of self. To hold on and maintain the false concept of who you are as you chant, is Prabhupada's definition of the tenth offense in chanting.

The Padma-parana describes the tenth offense as simply maintaining material attachment in spite of having been instructed that you are not the material mind or body. In other words, to maintain a false conception of yourself as the material mind and body with a story, is synonymous with maintaining material attachments.

There is a secondary aspect to the tenth offense mentioned in the padma-purana. Can you please read aloud in Chinese the description of the tenth offense that is written in the Vaishnava song book? Thank you.

*To not have complete faith in the chanting of the Holy Name and to maintain material attachments, even after understanding so many instructions on this matter. It is also an offense to be inattentive while chanting.*

In Prabhupada's version of the tenth offense, as stated in his C.C. purport, describes inattentive chanting slightly differently than in the song book. This is also very interesting. Prabhupada turns the definition around. Prabhupada describes inattention to the Holy Name as, *it is an offense if one does not show love and respect for chanting the Holy Name*. In other words, when you chant inattentively, you are not showing love or respect for the Holy Name. Conversely, when you chant with attention, or when you are present for the Holy Name, you are showing love and respect for the Holy Name.

If we are not chanting with respect and love, then we are chanting inattentively. If we are not present for Krishna in the form of His Holy Name, it is an offense.

If you maintain awareness of your true Self in the present, you will sense without effort that you are conscious and consciousness has a source. Your life has a source. When you are conscious of being conscious in the present, you can perceive directly that consciousness, life, has a source. Krishna is the cause of all causes. Remain self-aware as you chant the Holy

Name and you will spontaneously feel grateful for your life and the source of life, Sri Krishna. Then it can be said that you are chanting with genuine respect and love.

I encourage you to choose to be present for the Holy Name for at least three mantras at a time. This is doable for everyone. If after three mantras your attention becomes lost in thought, just notice it and bring your consciousness back to the Mahamantra again, just for another three mantras, and repeat.

When you are not chanting, make it your priority to live life in the present. You can accomplish this very easily. During the day, whenever you remember, just gently choose to be present with something that is present with you (like, your breath), become self-aware and thank Krishna for your life. Do this many times a day.

From Presence you will experience the real you; the light of consciousness that comes from Krishna. In this way, you will not be maintaining the material concept of life while you are chanting, or when you not chanting.

What is the cause of ignorance?

*A devotee answers: The want to control, want to enjoy.*

Guru replies: wanting to enjoy the illusion of maya and wanting to be in control are caused by ignorance. But what causes ignorance?

*Another devotee answers: Pride.*

Guru replies: Yes, pride is also an outcome of ignorance.

*Another devotee says: Lack of real knowledge.*

Guru replies: Lack of knowledge is the same as ignorance. What causes ignorance?

*Another devotee answers: Forgetting Krishna...*

Guru replies: Yes, ignorance is to forget our true self and our relationship with Krishna. How does that happen? Being forgetful of our true self and our relationship with Krishna is happening all the time. Forgetfulness of God doesn't happen just one time in the distant past. We forget our true self and Krishna moment to moment.

This is it. I found the verse, SB 11-2-37. I will come back to this discussion of the cause of ignorance in a moment.

*Fear arises when a living entity misidentifies himself as the material body because of absorption in the external, illusory energy of the Lord. When the living entity thus turns away from the Supreme Lord, he also forgets his own constitutional position as a servant of the Lord. This bewildering, fearful condition is brought about by the potency for illusion, called māyā. Therefore, an intelligent person should engage unflinchingly in the unalloyed devotional service of the Lord, under the guidance of a bona fide spiritual master, whom he should accept as his worship-able deity and as his very life and soul.*

The Guru shows an example by asking one disciple to stand up, looking at each other.

Now I'm giving my full attention to you, which is my presence (the disciple), and you are giving your presence of attention to me, so we are actually giving each other full attention. But if I go like this (Guru turns his head away), what am I doing? I'm ignoring her.

Actually, in English, the word *ignorance* comes from the word *to ignore*. As living beings, in essence, we all are beings of consciousness, right? I have this free will that I can put my conscious attention wherever I want. So, I have the choice to be conscious of you or not, to love you or not. Giving your conscious attention to someone is an act of love. It is my choice to love you, to be present with you, or not; and you can't do anything about it. Otherwise, without choice there can be no love, right? We have to have a choice to love or not, otherwise love is forced.

When consciousness is lost in thought and at the same time we are chanting, we are not present. We are unconscious of ourself as a being of awareness. We are ignoring our true self and we are ignoring Krishna in the form of the sound of His name. Being lost in the mind and daydreaming is a form of ignorance. Ignorance arises from the act of ignoring the reality of the present. We have a choice to be present for Krishna or not.

So, I like this verse because it perfectly describes our disease of ignorance and the cure for this disease. This is the verse that I was trying to find a few moments ago but couldn't. I said it will come to me later, but I didn't really believe that it would, but it did. Thank you Paramatma.

This verse is spoken by one of the Navayogendras, who are the sons of Rishabhdeva. Lord Caitanya quoted this verse when He was describing the dilemma of the soul to Sanatana Goswami.

C.C. Madhya-Lila 20.119

*bhayaṁ dvitīyābhiniveśataḥ syād īśād apetasya viparyayo 'smṛtiḥtan-māyayāto budha ābhajet taṁ bhaktyaikayeśaṁ guru-devatātmā*

*When the living entity is attracted by the material energy, which is separate from Kṛṣṇa, he is overpowered by fear. Since he is separated from the Supreme Personality of Godhead by the material energy, his conception of life is reversed. In other words, instead of being the eternal servant of Kṛṣṇa, he becomes Kṛṣṇa's competitor. This is called viparyayo 'smṛtiḥ. To nullify this mistake, one who is actually learned and advanced, worships the Supreme Personality of Godhead as his spiritual master, worshipful deity and source of life. He thus worships the Lord by the process of unalloyed devotional service.'*

The verse states that as soon as we ignore our real self as a servant of the Lord, we feel disconnected from the Lord. Conversely, when we are conscious in the present moment, we feel connected to our real self, God, and everything that expands from God. When we are not present, we feel disconnected, which is ignorance because at no time can we ever be separated from the Lord. Can a ray of the sun ever exist separated from the sun?

Due to ignorance, one becomes identified with the material body and absorbed into the Maya energy of illusion. When the living entity turns away from the Lord, he forgets his connection to the Lord as the Lord's servant; and then this fearful condition arises. I am alone. I have to protect myself. I am going to die. Therefore, an intelligent person should engage himself in the service of the Lord, and turn his face (attention) back to the Lord. In other words, the cure for ignorance is to correct the cause of ignorance. Choose to stop ignoring your true self and your relationship with God.

This verse of Srimad Bhagavatam informs us that we can stop ignoring the Lord by choosing to bring our conscious attention back to the Lord in three ways. We turn our face (or attention) back to the Lord by appreciating Guru as the external manifestation of the Lord of the heart, who appears in our life to guide us on the path of awakening Bhakti. We can acknowledge the presence of the Lord within our heart as the source of life, and we can also worship the Lord in the heart as the source of life.

We acknowledge the Lord every time we feel alive in the present and thank the divine source. By acknowledging the Lord's presence in these three ways, we reverse the cause of ignorance. Ignorance is resolved by acknowledging the Lord instead of ignoring Him. We acknowledge the Lord every time we choose to be present and thank God for the gift of life.

Ignorance arises when we ignore the truth of life, when we are not present. There are only two possibilities. We can choose to be here and awake in the present, or we can choose to not be here, or lost in the world of thought. The opposite of ignoring is to be attentive and conscious of being conscious.

Love is a conscious choice to turn our conscious gaze back to the Lord. We accomplish this by choosing to be present in the truth of life and hear the sound vibration of the Holy Name. By choosing to be present for Krishna when we chant, we avoid the tenth offense in chanting. We are attentive and peacefully without extra effort transcend the bodily concept of life.

As a human being, we have the gift of self-awareness that allows us to choose to be present or not. When we chant, we have this fundamental choice to be present for the Holy Name or not. Until we learn to distinguish the difference between being awake in the present and being lost in thought, we really don't have a choice to be present in the truth of life and present for Krishna's Holy Name. But, once we have been educated by an awakened being and have thus discovered the doorway to awakening that is always available in the present moment, we are free to choose between these two very different worlds. Begin by choosing to be present with something that is present with you. Gradually you will certainly awaken out of the illusory world of the mind into the reality of life now, and experience the joy of being and deepen your relationship with the Supreme Being.

Here is the choice. Will you maintain the false self by daydreaming about the past and future, or will you choose to live in the real self and be present for Krishna in the form of His Holy Name? As human beings, we potentially have this choice; and if we chant the Holy Name with respect and love, we will be attentive because the Lord is there in the sound vibration. I always recommend, just like I always recommend to those participants who attend the two-day seminars: stay present for 3 breaths. I recommend to the devotees to stay present for 3 mantras. In this way you will not be inattentive while chanting, nor will you be maintaining a false concept of yourself. By the proper use of free will, you can correct the original mistake of ignoring the Lord.

When and how did we ignore the Lord? The answer to this question, according to my research is that, we don't know exactly. We know we have fallen from grace. Somehow or other we ignored the absolute truth, and for a great many people ignoring the truth of life continues on, moment to moment.

The fall of the *Jiva-atma* (eternal spark of consciousness) is a great Mystery. The fall of the *Jiva-atma* into ignorance is a hotly debated topic even amongst devotees within Caitanya Vaishnavism. But why should the fall of the *Jiva-atma* matter to us at this point in our journey in the material world? One thing we do know for certain is that we are here in this world. How we got here is irrelevant. Somehow or other we are caught in ignorance. We are fallen. Somehow or other we are continuing to ignore the Lord and resist His Supreme authority. Therefore, we are designated as fallen souls.

We don't know exactly how or when we fell into ignorance. How and when we fell does not matter now. What is of critical importance for us now is to take the remedy and correct our mistake. A man falls off a pier into the ocean and is drowning. What must he do now? We are drowning in an ocean of ignorance. That is an undeniable fact. What is most important for us to do now? Choose to awaken and correct our mistake of ignoring the Lord by deciding to stop ignoring Him. We choose Presence. We choose to stay awake in the truth of life. If we properly utilize our free will to stop ignoring our true self and our relationship with the Lord of our life, we will come out of ignorance. We will awaken and transcend the false ego.

It is a choice you must make moment to moment. Each moment, choose to be conscious of being conscious and you will be free of the cycle desire and hate, which is born out of the false identity with matter. Each moment you are awake in the present you transcend the fear of death, abhiniveshata.

In the transliteration of the above verse from Srimad

Bhagavatam, Abhiniveshata, means because of the absorption in separation; abhini means separate. If you imagine that you are different in quality from the Lord or exist independent of the Lord, from this illusion of separation, arises fear bhayam).

Have you heard the word Abhaya, Abhaya Caran? Somebody very famous is named Abhaya Caran, the abbreviation is A.C. (devotees then realized it was Prabhupada's name).

*One devotee asks: You've mentioned 3 ways in which devotees acknowledge the presence of the Lord. One is through Guru, another is through seeing the Lord within one's heart, what about the third way?*

Guru replies: Thank you, the third way is seeing the Lord in the external form of the deity and internally as the source of your life.

You can see the deity in three ways. You can see your Guru as a deity, as the external form of Lord coming to enlighten and save you. In other words, the Lord comes to us through these three ways: as Guru, as the external and internal object of worship, and as the source of life that exists at the centre of being at the heart of consciousness. So, we turn our attention to the Lord in those three ways - seeing the Lord externally as Guru, the deity, and internally as the Super-soul who is the very source of life. In this way we correct the original mistake of ignoring the Lord.

Now, is your understanding of the tenth offense a little different than before? So, what is your understanding now? When you consider the tenth offense, what comes to your mind now? What images are there?

*A devotee answers: Not ignoring anything in the environment.*

Guru says: Ok. Just share your understanding now. What is your understanding of tenth offense? What does it mean to you?

*Another devotee answers: My understanding of tenth offense is to chant in presence, and to change my identification with the false self in my mind. For, over lifetimes the identification is so deep, so to change it I have to really make great efforts, and experience many challenges.*

*Another devotee answers: To really change my heart.*

*Another devotee answers: The main thing is to not be inattentive in chanting, and really focus on Krishna during the chanting.*

Guru replies: When we chant with respect and love, that means we chant with awareness of the presence of Holy Name, just like we are aware of each other's presence in this room.

*Another devotee says: The Nectar of Instruction says we should think of Krishna 24X7, but for people like me who live in the city, we are bewildered by the Maya. So, most of our time is spent being attached to the material, but if we are really determined to chant, try to do service 24 hours, then we are making a commitment to Krishna, promising that we are renouncing our false ego in the present moment, and focus all our mind on Krishna. Through the connection with Krishna and chanting, we will achieve peace of mind and endless joy within. If at this moment we are distracted, then it's disrespect to Krishna, and also not taking our commitment seriously.*

*Another devotee says: My new understanding is that the advancement in spiritual life is not how many efforts we have made through services, but actually, how many desires we have given up. How much identification with the false self has been given up?*

Guru replies: When I hear this *"giving up material desires"*, it sounds somewhat artificial, it's not the real thing. The real thing is when you get a higher taste, you lose the lower taste. Of course, we have to control the mind and senses, but we can't expect the fire of material desire to go out if we pour gasoline on the fire at the same time by continuously daydreaming of how to become happy in the future.

So, we are allowed a reasonable amount of sense gratification, regulated sense gratification. Whatever we eat, whatever we do, we offer first to Krishna and receive His prasadam.

Krishna says we must regulate the senses in order to control them. Regulate means you have your dog on a leash. You allow your dog to go here and there, but not too far. Actually, Krishna says this is how you control the mind and senses.

I don't want to take up too much time, but there's a wonderful verse in the 11th canto that touches on this point. Krishna says you have to hold the leash in a balanced way - not too long and not too short - and this will lead to proper mind control. We have to watch the mind from presence so that we can know what the mind is doing. Our watchful eye is the leash. Otherwise, the doggie-like mind is without a leash and will by default continue to repeat its conditioned patterns of thinking, feeling and willing.

As you engage in Bhakti yoga, you will realize the real you. This direct experience of the truth of who you are is the beginning of the higher taste Krishna talks about in BG 2.59.

*"Though the embodied soul may be restricted from sense enjoyment, the taste for sense objects remains. But, ceasing such engagements by experiencing a higher taste, he is fixed in consciousness."*

As that taste increases, material attachment loses its appeal. It is like, if you bring me a plate of Prasadham right now, I can't eat because I'm already full. When you get a higher taste, you automatically feel whole and complete. You are at peace and feel happy just to be here. Life in this moment is enough. You are no longer seeking something more than life in this moment because you feel fully satisfied just to be alive in this moment by the grace of Krishna. Sat-Chit-Ananda is our eternal nature. As you become conscious of being, material attachments will automatically decrease without you having to artificially endeavour to renounce them.

For the devotee who is awake in the present, external objects like family, friends, house, car, job, and money do not become obstacles to remaining self-realized in your eternal identity as an eternal servant of Krishna. You belong to Krishna and everything & everyone belongs to Krishna. How can you renounce what does not belong to you?

At the same time, you have to become the master of your mind and senses. You cannot expect to awaken to the truth of who you are and at the same time, allow your attention to wander anywhere & everywhere like a dog off-leash.

As you discover the truth of being that is revealed in the present, you also see that Krishna is present in everything present. Nothing can exist without God. As you awaken in the present, you no longer see yourself or anything or anyone as separate from Krishna. You see everything is part of Krishna and you feel whole, no separation. You serve Krishna from a feeling of completeness and gratitude. Pure Bhakti is service without expectation for anything in return.

## Q & A:

*One devotee says: My spiritual practice is still very superficial, there's not much realization.*

Guru replies: Thank you for your honest confession. Being completely honest is one of the most critical steps on the path of awakening out of illusion. It took me twenty years to finally admit that I had not made much progress in chanting and that I had not had a direct experience of my true self. I knew a lot about spiritual concepts but hadn't realized the knowledge. I did not begin to see improvement in chanting and awakening until I was able to admit my lack of progress to myself, Guru and God. I also believe that honest admission of what we don't know, is preparation for knowing.

This purport that we are reading today, I had read previously three or four times since the Caitanya-caritāmṛta came out in 1975 or 1976. One day it just struck me how illuminating and clarifying these sublime words of Prabhupada were as I read the explanation of ten offenses contained in this purport. I noticed that Prabhupada's translation of the tenth offense in particular is profoundly specific and concise as compared to the translation of the tenth offense stated in the song book. The Padma-parana is written originally in Sanskrit and the verses in the Vaishnavas song book are the English translation of those verses.

Until I read this purport, my understanding of the meaning of the tenth offense was muddled and abstract, which made it difficult for me to practically avoid this offense. I did not understand that to maintain material attachment was synonymous with the mental habit to hold on to a false conception of myself. My consciousness was 100% lost in the mind. By constantly moving around between the past / future world of the mind, I was maintaining the false ego of *I and mine*. I was almost never present. I was addicted to thinking and fantasizing about past and future and did not even know it!

Here is the critical point to understand. We cannot actually serve Krishna and at the same time be imagining ourselves to be a separate ***doer*** that exists independent of Krishna. We can only serve Krishna from the recognition that ***I exist only because of***

***Krishna***. The true self is eternally connected with and dependent upon Krishna. I exist only because Krishna exists. I have no independent existence. I am a servant of Krishna. This is a fact.

The root cause of frustration in chanting is that a person chants the Holy Names, worships deities, reads scriptures etc. and follows the rules and regulations but does not actually surrender to the Supreme Lord. Instead, we perform the external actions of Bhakti with the false ego that *I am the doer.* BG. 3.27

*"The spirit soul bewildered by the influence of false ego thinks himself the doer of activities that are in actuality carried out by the three modes of material nature."*

Therefore, the first lesson taught by the spiritual master is that we do not belong to this material world. Actually, the true self is the servant of the servants of the servants of Supreme Lord Gopinath. All actions done with the feeling that, *I am the doer,* is something other than Bhakti. So obviously we will not experience the result of Bhakti until we are truly performing Bhakti.

Like I said, I joined the movement when I was 19. I chanted, studied the books and served Prabhupada's ISKCON movement whole heartedly for 20 years. But after 20 years, it became painfully obvious to me that I was still stuck in my mind and had not realized my true self or God. I understood the theory of the teaching but I had not realized it. The truth spoken of in the scriptures had not yet become real in my experience. I had to admit that I had not progressed in Bhakti and I was not happy.

Furthermore, I had to honestly admit that I was unhappy. During my conscious wakeful hours of the day, I was mostly daydreaming, lamenting the past and imagining happiness in the future. I had to admit that I had a lot of old, unresolved issues from the past that still consumed my attention. I could see that I was even trying to avoid, ignore, and escape old repressed pain by chanting. Frequently, my motivation for chanting was to gain relief from the suffering of an unhappy past or attain happiness in the imagined future. I was perpetually lost in thought, strategizing how to obtain happiness in the future as I chanted. In this way, as I chanted, I was maintaining the false conception of myself and material attachments.

The true self is eternal by nature; the self exists in the eternal present and can only be found here and now. Searching for the truth of who you are, keeps your consciousness lost in the past / future world of the mind. Avoidance of the now and seeking future attainment is a false ego strategy that effectively keeps us from awakening. Thus, the dilemma: we are seeking what we already are. You and I are already eternally conscious beings, always have been, always will be. BG 2.20

*"For the soul, there is neither birth nor death at any time. He has not come into being, does not come into being, and will not come into being. He is unborn, eternal, ever-existing and primeval. He is not slain when the body is slain."*

This admission of my lack of spiritual realization, even after many years of diligent practice, caused me to have a great doubt. Basically, doubts can arise from three categories. We may have all three doubts, or one or two. We might doubt our teacher, we might doubt the teaching, or we might doubt our own ability to get the results of the teaching. So, it is possible for us to have all three doubts, or two doubts, or just one of them.

Whenever we doubt, we stop moving forward. For example, when the sun goes down and it is dark outside, all of a sudden there is no light and you cannot see your next step forward. If all of the sudden there is darkness, we will stop walking and become afraid to move because we cannot see what is in front of us. Perhaps you hear a loud sound and you stop and feel afraid because you don't see what caused the noise or where the sound is coming from.

In my case, I didn't really doubt my teacher, Srila Prabhupada, but I did have doubts about the level of attainment in Krishna Consciousness that my God-brothers and God-sisters had reached. I was thinking, well, *I was pretending for 20 years to be happy, so they are probably pretending just like me. I didn't realize the philosophical truths, so they didn't realize the truth either.*

This is a kind of envious thinking. I didn't doubt Prabhupada was a realized soul. I didn't doubt the teaching of Lord Caitanya. However, I doubted my ability to properly apply the teaching and get the result.

So, I thought maybe it is possible that a few of my godbrothers and sisters are becoming self-realized, but I am not. That admission, *I have not yet realized the true self or become truly happy*, was a step forward for me. *The problem is with me*, I thought.

I understood that there isn't something deficient with the spiritual method of chanting God's name. Rather the problem was with the way I applied the method. In science, you can demonstrate the method is true if you apply the method properly and you get the same result every time.

Around the same time that it began to dawn on me that my chanting was substandard and that was the cause of my lack of spiritual progress, serendipitously, I mysteriously came upon an insightful clue that revealed to me a way forward. The clue was the instruction I exactly needed to know at that time of my greatest confusion and despair. I desperately wanted to know how I could improve the quality of my chanting and awaken spiritually.

The solution to my spiritual crisis appeared to me in a letter Prabhupada had written in 1958. The contents of the letter shed light on my dilemma and gave me simple and clear guidance as to how to proceed on the spiritual path. In my classes, I've often shared the profound teaching contained in that particular Srila Prabhupada letter.

I am paraphrasing —Prabhupada wrote: *Happiness is within everyone and you have to learn how to introspect within yourself in order to find real happiness. Actually, in that letter Prabhupada didn't mention anything about chanting. Nevertheless, Prabhupada emphasized that if you want to awaken and be happy, you must learn how to look within. He also said that you will know if you are progressing or not on the spiritual path by your own direct experience.*

After reading that letter, I understood that I didn't know how to look within. I didn't know what looking within really meant. I did not know the way to look within. How I should go about it? Of course, I understood the words but had no personal experience of the meaning of the phrase, *to look within*. Right then and there, I resolved that if that is the direction I needed to go - to look within - then it was essential for me to learn how to journey within myself.

After reading Prabhupada's letter, I was convinced that I needed to learn how to introspect. After all, in his letter Prabhupada had emphasized the necessity of introspection so strongly. I wasn't sure how to proceed on this path. So, I prayed to be guided.

Mysteriously and innocently, I began to sit in silence every morning for about an hour with a timer. Intuitively I was directed to simply look within by keenly observing thoughts, emotions and bodily sensations and just watch. The thoughts, emotions and sensations seemed to appear and disappear out of nowhere. I just knew that I was to allow whatever thoughts, emotions and sensations to arise until they passed away on their own accord without trying to control them. I cannot find more appropriate words to describe how I was guided in this process of introspection.

Perhaps, looking within is just too simple. Somehow or other I knew to just be present with whatever thought, emotion and sensation arose in the moment within my mind & body and allow the thoughts and feelings into the light of awareness. Just be here with whatever is here.

I was like a copper wire that does not resist the electrical current flowing through it. The key is to notice resistance (the feeling of wanting and not wanting) and then relax. Allow the hurt feeling, allow the judgmental thoughts, allow *without believing in the mental story* the feelings are telling you.

Simply, I would sit in silent presence an hour a day and observe thoughts, feelings and sensations without judgment or trying to control those thoughts, emotions and sensations. Very soon, just like awakening from dream, I saw clearly the distinction between thinking and awareness. I became self-aware in the present as a silent watcher. For the first time in my life, I experienced the joy of being. I understood Krishna's words, Kshetra-jna, the knower of the field.

Gradually, I applied living in the present to chanting with attention. I made a conscious choice to be present for Krishna's Holy Name as I chanted. From the vantage point of Presence, I could see clearly that life only exists now and that Krishna is the source of life. Naturally and spontaneously, I wanted to chant Krishna's name out of a feeling of gratitude for all that God does for me and for us.

Now, I teach the same process of introspection and letting go to whoever is interested. This class today is really a synopsis of my personal experience of the journey within. The journey within is a road we all must travel if we are to awaken out of the dream-world of the mind and into the reality of life revealed through the doorway of the present. The soul is eternally present because Krishna is eternally present, and therefore it is only in the present that you can find your true self and Krishna.

Srila Prabhupada's definition of the tenth offense in chanting in this purport brings such clarity to what it really means to maintain material attachment. After awakening in the present, in hindsight, I could understand that I had been committing the tenth offense all the years I had been chanting. For twenty years, I had been chanting Hare Krishna, and at the same time I was lost in the illusory world of the mind and maintaining the bodily concept of life.

The defect wasn't with the Holy Name, or the process of chanting. The defect was in the way I was attempting to chant. I wasn't present. Although I was physically present as I chanted, my conscious attention was somewhere else. I was lost in thought. I was wanting to be there, or

somewhere other than here. I wasn't present for Krishna as I chanted His Holy Name. I was ignoring Krishna as I chanted!

I can't comment or have an opinion concerning the quality of anyone else's chanting. I am just admitting to you. I can honestly say, for twenty years, I was not able to chant attentively. I was not present for Krishna when I was chanting. Even as I chanted, my consciousness was absorbed in the mind and maintaining a false conception of myself. Even as I chanted, my consciousness was lost in thought about the past and future. Unknowingly, I was maintaining the false identification with this body and mind with its illusory a story. So, it is not at all surprising that in spite of chanting for many years, practically I remained spiritually asleep and desperately unhappy.

Sadly, I did not actually understand and follow the very first instruction I received from Prabhupada. His first instruction to me was simple and very short. It was so simple that it seemed normal, but actually, I understand only now that his words were very profound.

Prabhupada gave me an instruction about a week after our first meeting in Tokyo. Although I was able to see him every day, and go on morning walks, etc., I did not have the opportunity to talk personally with Prabhupada until the day he was leaving Tokyo for India. This was in August of 1970. Prabhupada was travelling from America to India and he stopped in Japan for two weeks along the way. He was going to India to start the movement there, because there were no temples, and no ISKCON devotees in India at that time.

The week in Tokyo with Prabhupada came to the end. All the devotees went to the airport with Prabhupada, and we sat together in the VIP Lounge waiting for his flight to depart. In the VIP room, there was a big round sofa and Prabhupada was sitting on the sofa. All of his disciples sat on the floor around his lotus feet. Then Prabhupada looked at me, and he went like this (Guru gestured), Prabhupada gestured with his hand that I should come sit next to him on the cushion. So, I went and sat on the sofa next to Prabhupada. He asked me, "what do your parents think about Krishna Consciousness?" It was the question that Prabhupada often asked his new disciples. So Prabhupada made an effort to have a conversation with me, which made me feel comfortable and not so nervous. In reality, I was petrified. I answered Prabhupada, "my parents don't know anything about Krishna, but I think they would like that I am becoming a devotee because my parents always support me in whatever I want to do." This was true. Prabhupada smiled and said, "that's very nice."

Then he asked me, "so, do you like chanting Hare Krishna?" At that time, I really did; it was so new. Hence, I honestly said, "yes, I like chanting Hare Krishna." Then Prabhupada smiled and said to me, "if you always chant Hare Krishna, Hare Krishna,

Krishna Krishna, Hare Hare, Hare Rama, Hare Rama, Rama Rama, Hare Hare, you will always be happy."

It seems like a simple statement, right? But are we always chanting Hare Krishna? Are we genuinely chanting? Or are we somewhere else when we are chanting? Prabhupada's words were grave and deeply meaningful. Prabhupada's statement was a divine instruction. All of my life, those words of Srila Prabhupada have remained fresh within my mind and supported me, even though I could not follow or understand his instruction. I can say that when I was actually chanting Hare Krishna, I was happy; and when I wasn't truly chanting Hare Krishna, I wasn't happy. So, we really have to be here for Krishna, we have to be present when we chant. We always have a choice to be here, or, to be somewhere other than here. We have the awesome power of free will. No one can force us. We can put our attention anywhere we choose.

Your mind might say, "it is really difficult to be present". Is that a true statement? To be present is really a simple choice. We can always choose to bring our attention into the reality of the present moment, just for now, just for now, and just for now.

Perhaps the most important step you can take to awaken out of illusion and into the truth of life is often remember to intentionally, but gently, choose to be conscious of being conscious in the present. This is especially true if you do not feel you are making the kind of spiritual progress you were expecting.

To be awake in the present is just a simple choice. Since it is a simple choice, you cannot even consider living in the present to be a practice. It is too simple. The more you choose to be present, the more you will discover the truth of who you are in relationship to God. There is no permanent state of presence because you always have a choice.

To remain awake in the present is more of a process and a skill that develops over time. However, to be present is instantaneous. It is very simple and easy. You just simply choose to be present with anything that is present with you in this moment - like your breath, or the sounds you hear.

As soon as you bring your attention to the present, thoughts stop without you trying to stop them. You immediately come out of your mind and out of your story. You come out of the false conception you have of yourself; because mind is always about past / future. The false sense of self only exists in the mind when you think about past and future. From presence, you can awaken from the dream state and transcend your mind and all misconceptions. Learning to be present is the stepping stone for further spiritual advancement and supports pure chanting of the Holy Name.

I am not suggesting that thinking is not necessary or needs to be stopped. The purpose of the mind is to think. Do you even know what your next thought is going to be? In order to awaken spiritually, there is no need to stop thinking. However, you must know that thoughts are not real and that reality, life, consciousness, only exists in the present. There is no problem with thinking. Thinking is required while you are working, etc. If there is no need to think - such as when you are taking a walk or going to the toilet - then choose to be present and aware of your life for a few moments. When you are chanting, just hear the sound vibration and stay conscious of being conscious. Enjoy all that God is giving you in this moment. Appreciate the fullness and abundance of life in this moment as you chant.

Our motivation for choosing to be present is very simple. We choose to be alert and self-aware in the present because it is only in the present that you can experience the reality of life and the joy of being. As a human being you are always free to make this choice to live in the truth of life now. That's it! Simple.

Once you know that life in the mind is not real, you will choose to be present whenever you do not need to think. Thinking about the past and the future are useful only to the degree that it helps you deal with the present. Only life now is real. Choose to be present many times a day, especially when you chant. The more you choose to be present, the more you will experience the fact that the only life you really have is now.

*One devotee asks: If I really spend a certain period of time just chanting, nothing else, will I make a breakthrough?*

Guru answers: That depends upon the quality of your chanting. What determines the quality of your chanting? Your degree of presence. As soon as you choose to be present and you become present with something that is present, like the Tulsi plant for example, you are in that moment an awakened being. You have come out of the mind, out of your story. You are self-aware in the present moment. That is a real breakthrough.

When you are present, you break identification with your mind and come to a higher level of consciousness. By direct experience you understand the difference between reality of life in the present and the illusionary world of thought. If you are present for the Holy Name as you chant, then you will certainly break through the illusion of Maya. You will become spiritually steady and from the stage of steadiness you will develop a taste for the Holy Name.

What do you mean by the word *break through*? The egoistic mind is always looking for more, seeking something special, wanting something other than the life Krishna is already giving in this moment. The life gifted by Krishna is eternally complete. Everything that emanates from the complete whole, Krishna, is already complete. Life in the present is complete. You already are what you seek.

As long as we seek more than what Krishna is giving right now, we cannot be present to experience completeness. In order to seek, you have to go into your mind and imagine attainments and happiness in the future. If you cannot be present, you cannot experience the perfection of life that is already within you. Without rapt attention, you cannot perceive the presence of Krishna in the sound of the Holy Name. You and I and everyone are already eternally complete parts of Krishna. The experience of the joy of being and your eternal connection to Krishna is available to you right now in this present moment. We just have to choose it.

You might be chanting many rounds, even for a long period of time, but if you are not present for the sound of the Holy Name while chanting, then you will continue to be lost in thought and unaware of your true being. Unless you are present, you cannot distinguish reality from illusion. You cannot distinguish the real you from the false you. Until you awaken in the present, real happiness will elude you. In this regard, the quality of chanting is more important than quantity.

After the Padma-purana lists the 10 offenses, it says, via continuous chanting one will eventually overcome the offenses in chanting. However, the Padma-purana doesn't say when you will have a breakthrough, or come to the offense-less stage of chanting. How long is a long time?

Regarding the chanting, the quality of chanting is more important than the quantity. You can chant for lifetimes and if you are still committing the ten offenses to the Holy Name, the seed of Bhakti does not sprout.

Prabhupada has given us the proper quantity of rounds to chant daily, so that must be the right prescription. A minimum of sixteen rounds a day is Guru's order. If you follow Guru's order, Krishna is pleased. It is all Guru and Krishna's mercy. If we do our best to follow the Guru's order, Krishna accepts our chanting. Chanting sixteen rounds is our main service to Guru and Krishna. Krishna honours the order of the Guru. Krishna is pleased when we follow Guru's order to chant sixteen rounds.

When we chant, we are not expecting joy for ourselves. We are simply trying to please Guru and Krishna. The result is up to them. Pure Bhakti is the only thing that is pleasing to Krishna. Krishna's pleasure is the main ingredient for success. Being willing to do what is pleasing to Krishna is how we make progress in Bhakti. When Guru and Krishna are pleased, revelation of the absolute truth awakens in our consciousness by Divine grace only.

Now, whether you sit down to chant all sixteen rounds at one time, or you break it up into sessions, the quality of hearing of each mantra, of each round, continues to be of paramount importance. I witnessed Prabhupada chanting some of his rounds in the evening time when he stayed in Hawaii.

In 1975, Prabhupada was in Hawaii for a month finishing his writing of the Caitanya-caritāmṛta. Every night I brought him hot milk and, in the evening, when I brought him hot milk, I noticed that Prabhupada was walking around in his room chanting on his beads.

Later on, I confirmed with Prabhupada's personal servant: Prabhupada's normal routine was to chant 4 rounds before Mangala Aarti, 4 rounds after Mangala Aarti, and he would chant 4 rounds after breakfast or in the afternoon, and then 4 rounds in the evening.

Somehow or other, whenever we chant, we should have the intention to chant as attentively as possible. If we are committed to living in the present during the times we are not chanting, we are more likely to be attentive to the Holy Name when we are chanting. We want to be present for Krishna in the form of His divine name whenever we chant.

Everyone has a different work schedule. Our life progresses through different phases from youth, to midlife, to old age. So, we have to be flexible and be able to adjust the quality of our chanting to the time, place and circumstances of our life. If you are adept at living in the present, you will find that you can easily be present for Krishna wherever you are and whenever you chant.

I recommend to everyone: just decide to be present for 3 mantras as you chant. Let that be your goal. Then you will be present for most of each round. You will chant peacefully without becoming tired, bored or stressed out. Chanting becomes very steady and peaceful. You are grateful to Krishna and happy to be alive. You have no expectations and just totally depend upon Krishna.

Improve the quality of your chanting and you will have a breakthrough. The first breakthrough is to realize the distinction between thinking and awareness. You realize, *I am spirit, I am pure consciousness.* By consciously choosing to be present during your day, you will awaken spiritually very quickly. You are already an eternal being. No need to seek what you already are. What you truly are is revealed to you the more you choose to live in the present. When you are actually present, you will begin to perceive the truth of your being as the unchanging presence of awareness.

*One devotee asks: The essence of Mahaprabhu's philosophy is simultaneously one and different, with regards to our relationship with the Supreme Lord. Somehow, we ignored Him, hence in this material world, "One" with the Lord is that we are never separate from the Lord, and when we are present, we feel that we are not separate from Him. Afterwards it will automatically manifest within all the knowledge regarding "being different with the Lord". Therefore, first we realize that we are qualitatively the same as the Lord. Secondly, we realize that we are different from the Lord. Do I understand it right?*

Guru replies: The sun and the rays of light emanating from the sun are forever simultaneously the same and different. The sun and its rays are one in quality. The difference is that the sunray depends upon the sun as the source of existence. Similarly, when you are conscious of being conscious, you become conscious of your eternal and joyful quality, or Brahman nature. You can also simultaneously perceive that your existence is dependent upon the Supreme Brahman, Krishna. Even when we realize our true spiritual nature and oneness with God, we never lose the perception of ourselves as individual awareness. The progressive realization of the Absolute Truth is described in BG. 18.54

Brahma-bhuta prasannatma, By the art of yoga you separate pure consciousness from entanglement within the material mind and body and you begin to see your true self as the witnessing presence of awareness that is dependent upon the source of awareness, the Supreme Awareness. When consciousness is purified from identification with matter, pure Bhakti can begin.

According to the shastra, prior to entering the material world the *Jiva-atma* (soul) is situated in the body of Maha Vishnu. The *Jiva-atma* that exist in the body of Maha Vishnu, are not developed in the sense that there is no individual awareness of life, although each *Jiva-atma* is eternally an individual being. The *Jiva-atma* has a Svarupa (an eternal form), a form that loves God in a particular way. But the *Jiva-atma* present in the body of Maha Vishnu has no individual self-awareness; there is Brahman awareness or oneness consciousness. The svarupa of the *Jiva-atma* situated in the body of Mahavishnu is in a non-manifest state. The *Jiva-atma* exists in the body of MahaVishnu in a state of oneness consciousness.

Upon Mahavishnu's exhalation, the material universes expand from the pores of His body. The individual souls, or *Jiva-atma,* who are present in the body of Mahavishnu are then injected into the material world by His glance. The *Jiva-atma*, leave the body of Mahavishnu and are impregnated into the material world. The *Jiva-atma,* in contact with Maya, becomes conditioned by the three modes of matter and experiences the illusion of separation from God. The *Jiva-atma,* being conditioned by Maya, forgets the eternal connection of oneness with God.

The materially conditioned *Jiva-atma* under the influence of Maya feels cut off from the source of life and experiences overwhelming fear. By the influence of the mode of ignorance, the *Jiva-atma* assumes a false sense of self. The false ego imagines, *I exist separate from God and everything else.* The forgetful *Jiva-atma,* under the influence of the false ego, travels around the material universe from one material body to the next, in a continuous cycle of birth and death.

After many lifetimes in the material world, when the *Jivaatma* is fortunate, the conditioned soul receives the opportunity to come to the path of surrender to God. The *Jiva-atma* who has awakened faith in God, surrenders to

God and begins to chant the Holy Name. By surrender to God and chanting His name, the *Jiva-atma* becomes purified from identification with the false self. Gradually, the *Jiva-atma* discovers its true spiritual identity as pure individual consciousness, and that it is eternally connected with God in love as a dependent servant.

When a conditioned *Jiva-atma* begins the path of surrendering to God and chanting the Holy Name, it is still in ignorance and is not conscious of being conscious. The unit of consciousness, *Jiva-atma*, is unaware of the true self. But as one chants and avoids the offenses, Cetodarpanam-marjanam, the consciousness of the *Jiva-atma* is purified of identification with the material mind and body. The *Jiva-atma* realizes, *I am not the mind or the body, I am eternal consciousness and servant of the divine. I am, but I have a source.* This is the awakening consciousness of simultaneous oneness and difference with God. *I am because God is.*

By the yoga process of attentive chanting, *Jiva-atma* experiences a growing internal self-aware. It has direct experience of self-awareness; *I am this unchanging presence of awareness.* All fear disappears and the certainty of eternal existence awakens within as one continues to chant. *I am an individual point of pure consciousness that comes from God.*

Navigating this particular section of spiritual awakening, that is between steadiness after purification and increasing taste for the Holy Name, can be a little awkward for some devotees. This is because the awakening *Jiva-atma* has not yet fully perceived his individual spiritual form, svarupa, or the form of the

Lord. The *Jiva-atma* realizes that it is pure spiritual energy but is not aware of its spiritual form yet.

As we progress in spiritual awareness, we awaken to this awareness of our individual self that is eternal, and at the same time we feel connected to and dependent upon the source of consciousness, the Supreme Consciousness. This is Paramatma realization.

Like right now, when you are present with something here that is present, the mind falls silent and your experience is of the silent presence of awareness, or what we call presence. In presence, even though your mind is silent, you don't lose awareness of yourself as an individual who is experiencing. Also, you don't feel separate or disconnected from the source of life. Both the experience of oneness and difference are there. There is the perception of oneness and difference. *I am because God is. I exist because God exists.*

As awareness is not an object, only awareness can be aware of awareness. Awareness is beyond the mind. When you were resting in the body of Mahavishnu, the perception of simultaneous oneness and difference with God was not yet awakened in you. Before you came to the material world, you also had no perception of yourself as an individual. When you were existing in the body of Maha Vishnu, you had no awareness of the difference between you and God. You only perceived oneness. The perception of oneness and difference with God is only a potential for the *Jiva-atma* who exists within the body of MahaVishnu. The perception of oneness and difference with God wasn't known to you before you came into the material world.

The body of MahaVishnu is the transcendental spiritual dimension of existence or the spiritual world. When you existed in the body of MahaVishnu, you only knew a sense of oneness. Therefore, the *Jiva-atma's* coming to the material world is purposeful, and ultimately, God's will and design.

The individual consciousness of the *Jiva-atma* has been evolving in the material world, just as a plant evolves from a seed. Gradually, consciousness transforms from the experience of absolute oneness (the *Jiva-atma's* state of consciousness when existing in the body of MahaVishnu) to the illusion of absolute difference, *I am this mind and body, I am separate from God and everyone else,* that one experiencing as a conditioned soul in the material world. This is Maya consciousness; and, the consciousness of the *Jiva-atma* finally matures to the realization of simultaneous oneness and difference with God. *I am the eternal servant of God*. The *Jiva-atma,* with this matured consciousness oneness and difference, is qualified to engage in a loving relationship with the Supreme Lord. God's design and purpose of the material world has been fulfilled when the *Jiva-atma* awakens and surrenders to God.

On our journey in the material world, we awaken to our true self, that is revealed in the present. Eventually we come to perceive our oneness and difference with the source of Life, the cause of all causes, Sri Krishna. However, our journey is not yet complete. Our Svarupa (personal spiritual form) hasn't been revealed to us yet. Or, I should say, most of us in this room today have not yet realized our svarupa, one's eternal spiritual form. As we continue on the path of Bhakti, as given to us by the acharyas, we will certainly awaken to our full potential to love Krishna in our eternal spiritual body.

Whatever stage of devotion a devotee is on, if the devotee sincerely follows Guru and Krishna's instructions, he or she can be confident that Krishna is pleased. If Krishna is pleased, then our divine mission is being fulfilled. By the Lord's grace, His Bhakti shakti will reveal to us our spiritual form, which will enable us to see the Lord and serve Him personally.

Prabhupada wites in SB 8.5.24, purport:

*Lord Kṛṣṇa is very much pleased with His devotees, even if they are not on the topmost stage of devotional service. Even on the lower stages of devotional service one is transcendental, and if one continues with devotional life, he continues to be a deva or asura. If one continues in this way, Kṛṣṇa will always be pleased with him and will give him all instructions so that he may very easily return home, back to Godhead.*

Lord Caitanya asks everyone to chant Hare Krishna. In the beginning of chanting, the consciousness is cleansed. The dust on the mirror is removed, cheto-darpana-marjanam. The consciousness is cleared of the false material identity and the devotee realizes — *I am* — the pure light of consciousness that emanates from the Supreme Consciousness. From there, the connection with the Lord through chanting Hare Krishna deepens and we experience the Lord as the source of life. This awakening, *I am because*

*God is*, is the dawning of one's relationship in love with the

Lord and His Holy Name. It is a real and practical relationship, not at all theoretical. I know by direct experience that I exist because God exists. What could be more intimate? This elementary relationship with the Lord is expressed as *I am because God is*.

After consciousness is purified from identification with the material energy, when we are spiritually mature, the Svarupa shakti reveals to us our Svarupa, or spiritual form. We are blessed by the touch of the Svarupa shakti. Then we have a sense of our spiritual identity. From the awareness of our svarupa arises a personal feeling of love for the Lord in one of His many forms. Our personal attraction to the Lord awakens within us by the divine Grace of God. By the power of our love of God, we are granted spiritual eyes with which to see the personal form of the Lord. The purpose of our journey to the material world has been fulfilled. We can now engage in a loving relationship with God in oneness and difference consciousness.

This awakening, *I am the eternal presence of awareness,* occurs before we see the Lord. Before we see the Lord in the form of His name, we see our own eternal spiritual form, svarupa. This progressive realization is described in a letter written by Srila Bhaktisiddhanta Prabhupada. I'm not making this up.

This is a letter Bhakti Siddhanta Prabhupada wrote to one of his disciples. This letter describes the stages of realization we go through as we become purified by chanting Hare Krishna. The same progressive steps in

God realization are described by Lord Caitanya in His Siksashastakam.

*"I'm overjoyed to hear that your enthusiasm for chanting has increased, as our contaminations are removed by chanting, the Lord's form, quality and pastime will be revealed to us in the Holy Name."*

So, what happens first? Contaminations are removed; freedom from material identification occurs before realization of one's spiritual form. After purification of consciousness, one's spiritual form is revealed, followed by revelation of the Lord's form, quality and pastimes.

*"There's no point in making a separate effort to artificially remember the Lord's form, quality and pastime.*

You shouldn't be using mental effort to visualize. *(*Actually, trying to see the Lord is a subtle form of control being exerted by the false ego.*)*

*The Lord and His Name are one and the same; this will be understood clearly when the coverings on your heart are removed. By chanting without offenses, you will personally realize that all perfection comes from the Holy Name. Through chanting, the distinction that exists between the self and the gross body is gradually effaced. Gradually one realizes one's own spiritual form."*

According to Srila Bhakti Siddanta Thakur, the first transformation that results from chanting is the eradication of one's identification with the false self, mind, and material body. By direct experience your true identity as pure consciousness, *I am or I am spirit,* is clearly perceived. This is self-realization. Then you realize your spiritual form. Then you realize God's form. Bhakti Siddanta Thakur is explaining the progressive realization of the true self and God that occurs by chanting the Holy Name of the Lord.

*"Once you are aware of your spiritual body, as one continues to chant, one sees the transcendental nature of the Lord's form."*

So, we actually realize our own spiritual form before we perceive the Lord's form. However, we don't realize our spiritual form until we first awaken to the truth of who we are as an eternal conscious being, *I am. I am spirit.* We don't really realize pure consciousness until consciousness is purified from identification with the mind. Consciousness is in a pure state when one is awake in the present and giving full attention to the sound vibration of the Holy Name.

You can never lose your individuality. Even when you are present, even when you have the sense of oneness, you don't lose your sense of self as an individual unit of awareness. This *I am* never disappears.

For some of you, it may seem that in the beginning of your experience of Presence, you lose your sense of self. But actually, you are only losing the sense of a false self. This is because living in your mind under the control of the self-image, habitually thinking about past and future, has been the default mode of consciousness for lifetimes. Who are you without memories of the past? Who are you in this moment of now without your story? For lifetimes we have derived our sense of self from thinking about the past. When you are fully awake in the present, your self-image is absent because there are no thoughts. The false self only exists as a thought when we are thinking of past and future. So, for those who are new to living in the present, the absence of the false self can be a little disorienting.

We are so accustomed to deriving a sense of self, our identity, from our memory. Naturally, some people freak out when the mind is silent and there is only the perception of the presence of awareness. When you are present, there is no thought of past or future.

Therefore, when you are present there is no *self-image* present. This is because the self-image is no more than a fantasy based on the remembered the past. In the present, there are no thoughts about past or future. Without a past, who are you? *Without a past, I don't know who I am.*

In the beginning of the process of awakening, most people feel a little bewildered and unsettled when they begin to practice living in the present because their self-image is absent. For lifetimes we have derived our identity, our sense of "self", from thinking and remembering the past. Naturally, but mistakenly, some people feel the experience of Presence is impersonal or empty at first.

But on close examination you will notice that when you are awake in the present, you never lose your individuality as a unique point of awareness. The only thing empty about awakened Presence is that Presence is empty of the false ego. Gradually you will experience that Presence is not empty or impersonal, but rather you will feel full and complete. *I am pure consciousness* that comes from the Supreme consciousness, Krishna.

We can never lose our sense of individuality. That is just a myth. We are eternally spiritual individuals. Krishna says clearly in BG 15.7, we are eternally His parts.

*The living entities in this conditioned world are My eternal fragmental parts. Due to conditioned life, they are struggling very hard with the six senses, which include the mind.*

When you are present, you have a sense of oneness and connection to the source of life but you never lose awareness of your true self as an individual point of experience. You always have this sense of *I am*, I *am here, I am experiencing*. Awakened Presence, *Brahma-bhuta*, is actually the state of pure consciousness that leads to the entrance of pure Bhakti and the realization of oneness and difference.

You can't serve Krishna in the false conception you have been maintaining of yourself. Krishna describes the progressive realization of the true self and of God in the Bhagavad Gita.

*brahma-bhūtaḥ prasannātmāna*
*śocati na kāṅkṣati*
*samaḥ sarveṣu bhūteṣu*
*mad-bhaktiṁ labhate parām*

*One who is thus transcendentally situated at once realizes the Supreme Brahman and becomes fully joyful. He never laments or desires to have anything. He is equally disposed toward every living entity. In that state he attains pure devotional service unto Me.* BG 18.54

When we realize *I am* an individual unit of pure consciousness, we don't merge into the light or lose our eternal sense of personal existence. We experience connectedness and oneness with God and His creation, but we never lose the sense of *I am.* However, in the beginning of our awakening, when we have the realization of our true self that is revealed in the present, all we can perceive is *I am pure consciousness, I exist, I am*. Who is present? *I am*.

Our *Svarupa* (spiritual form) is yet to be revealed to us. We can only know our *Svarupa* after consciousness is purified from identification with thought. By the grace of the Lord, our *Svarupa* is revealed when we fully surrender to Him.

When we are present, we are not lamenting the past or hankering for anything in the future. We realize, *I am* an eternal being, and that we are the same as everyone else. In that state, Krishna says, you can enter into the state of pure Bhakti. When you are awake in the present, you can chant peacefully without offenses.

The pure chanting of God's name is the foundational teaching of Sri Caitanya Mahaprabhu. According to A.C.

Bhaktivedanta Swami Prabhupada and Bhaktisiddanta Thakur, the attainment of pure chanting develops progressively when chanting is performed with attention and respect. Sri Caitanya Mahaprabhu has stated that in this age of Kali, the source of all beings incarnates in the form of His Holy Name. Since the Supreme is present in the Holy Name, we demonstrate our respect and appreciation for the Holy Name when we are present for the Holy Name while chanting.

Inattentive chanting is a form of disrespect and neglect. Presence is the opposite of neglect. Presence is love. When we choose to be present for someone, we are telling them, *I respect you. I care about you enough to give you my full attention.* In response to the giving of our presence to another person, they naturally feel loved. Similarly, when we give our Presence to the Holy Name, the Lord appreciates our love.

Kali Kale Nama-Rupe Krishna-Avatar

Nama Haite haya sarva-jagat-nistara

C.C. Adi 17.22: *In the age of "Kali" Krishna descends in the form of his name. Anyone who takes shelter of the name becomes free from of the influences of this age of quarrel.*

Sri Caitanya Mahaprabhu also taught us,

*"If one chants the* Holy Name *of the lord again and again, yet his love for the Supreme lord does not develop, if tears do not flood his eyes, it is evident that because of his offenses to the* Holy Name *while chanting, the seed of Krishna Bhakti does not sprout. "*

For those of us who practice Bhakti-Yoga and mantra meditation, this teaching of Sri Caitanya is particularly important. In other words, if you do not feel genuinely happy when you repeat the mantra, it is painfully clear that you are not chanting with attention and respect. The lack of inner happiness as you chant is evidence that you are making offenses to the Holy Name. The most common offense and perhaps the most challenging to overcome, is inattention. If we are not present for Krishna in the form of His Holy Name as we chant, unfortunately, we are neglecting Him. If we are not present, then where are we? Lost in the mind, lost in an illusory self. Lost in lamentation and hankering.

One aim of these classes on the topic of Presence and Releasing is to assist yoga practitioners of Bhakti in becoming more attentive in all aspects of life, especially during the chanting of the Mahamantra. Bhaktivinod Thakur taught that the root cause of all the ten offenses is inattention. He also says that inattention is an expression of pride. Inattention and pride are the root cause of offensive chanting.

Bhaktivinod advises:

*"Forget the past that sleeps, and never future-dream at all, but act in times that are with thee and progress thee shall call."* Bhaktivinod/ Sara-grahi Vaishnava

***"Thought arises from cit-abhasa*** *and therefore it cannot be independent of the material elements. However, by stopping the functioning of the mind, a state of atmasamadhi can be induced in which the soul can be perceived. In other words, when we examine the soul through introspection, a direct spiritual perception of the soul can be obtained."* pg. 179 of Krsna – Samhita

Being self-aware in the present is the state of consciousness that Bhaktivinod Thakur calls atma-samadhi.

Learning to release identification with the false self and the illusory world of the mind, allows you to stay awake in the state of consciousness called atma-samadhi. The more you choose to live in the present, as Bhaktivinod Thakur suggests, the more you will realize the truth of who you are as pure consciousness. You are empowered by the truth within you. A higher level of consciousness has been activated. You are now the watcher of your mind and ego.

Simultaneously you also arise in mastery of your mind. This higher level of consciousness allows you to be happily present for Krishna as you chant anytime you choose.

Pride is a manifestation of the false ego. The false ego is an image we have of ourselves that is projected on the screen of our mind when we are thinking of the past and future. The false ego is a mentally-constructed false sense of self.

Before awakening, your home is the world of the mind, which is where most people live 100% of the time. You live in your self-created story, which is everything remembered from the past and everything imagined in the future. But when you are present, you come out of that story because the story is always about the past or future. The story is not real. When you are present, you come out of the dream world of the mind. In the dream, you imagine yourself to exist independent of the source of life and therefore experience fear and dissatisfaction. In your story, you sometimes overestimate yourself (pride) or underestimate yourself (doubt) - both are illusory and painful.

When you are lost in the mind and identified with thoughts, you imagine yourself to be separate from the source of life. It is like imagining that a ray of the sun, which is you, is piercing through the clouds and has somehow become separated from the sun. Mistakenly, you see the sunray to be separate from the sun. It is an optical illusion. Sometimes the clouds in the sky create such an optical illusion.

Our dream-self and its unhappy story does not exist in the now. The self-image is illusory. The self-image only appears to exist as past and future thoughts projected on the screen of the mind. The self-image moves within the mind between thinking of the past and the future. In the reality of the present, the imagined self with its feelings of pride and doubt disappears. When you are present, the mind falls silent and only pure awareness of existence is perceived.

What is in the story of our imagined self? The story begins in infancy. From conception in the womb and through early childhood development, our self-image was formed and includes a host of limiting false beliefs about ourselves, other people and the world. These acquired beliefs that are programmed into our mind from infancy are the fabric of the adult false ego we carry around today. *I am not good enough. I cannot do it. I am no good. I am not loved. There is no one here for me. I am all alone. I am stupid. Everyone is better than me. etc......*

Once those limiting beliefs are programmed into your mind, they colour your experience of life. For most people, who are not on the path of awakening, these beliefs remain active, conscious and unchallenged until death. Once you awaken, you can become conscious of the false ego and its limiting beliefs. It is only from the awakened state of presence that you can free yourself from the programmed illusory self-beliefs. From awakened self-awareness in the present, you can liberate yourself from your story and from the dream of separation from God. From present moment consciousness, you can transcend the illusory past and future world of the mind.

I once heard Mahatma Prabhu say, *"You can't just recognize your anarthas and do nothing about it."*

Pride often arises from the programmed false belief, *"I am not good enough."* The belief, *I am not good enough,* creates a horrible feeling of self-doubt and feeling of fear, which drives one to constantly try and prove to others, *"I am better than everyone else"*. Out of the fear of not being good enough arises the neurotic need to be special. This is the attitude of pride, which is a great obstacle to spiritual awakening and to authentic chanting.

Therefore, Mahaprabhu stresses from the beginning of His teaching that authentic chanting can only be performed with an attitude of humility. Humility is in direct opposition to the pride of the false ego. The false sense of self imagines that "I" exist independent of any source or higher power.

Therefore, the false self lives in a constant state of doubt and fear, which leads to obsessively trying to control one's external environment. The fearful false ego wants to control other people, places and things in order to feel safe and okay.

The false ego thinks, *only "I" can protect myself. I am alone.* As soon as one is awake in the present, however, one feels immediately safe, peaceful and connected. The competitive spirit born of fear dissolves into the light of humility and happiness that is emanating from the real self.

It is a mistake to believe that you don't have to attend to your *anarthas* and that *anarthas* will somehow magically dissolve. We must bring the *anartha* into the light of consciousness for healing and releasing in an inner environment humility and compassion. Notice it, allow it, feel it, admit it, confess it and then let go of it.

The illusory notion, "I" exist independent of the source of life, or a higher power, is not only the source of pride with in us; it is also the source of all material attachment. The illusion of separation from the source that is expressed as *"I exist independent of God"* is the cause of fear and the feeling of separation, which in turn creates a feeling of incompleteness. From this feeling of incompleteness flows all illusory attachment. When we feel incomplete, we experience the compulsive need to look outside ourself for the feeling of completeness and fulfilment.

Material attachment doesn't just mean being attached to social position, wife, family, home, job, nice car, etc. These are external attachments. What about more subtle attachments? *I want to be special, adored, the centre of attention, in control of others, and possess as much as possible.* When we are lost in the mind, we cannot feel our true life that exists now. We feel incomplete and disconnected from the source of life. Not being present and unaware of the truth of our life "now" leads to worrisome feelings, pride and all varieties of material attachment.

When consciousness becomes identified with thinking about past and future, consciousness becomes unconscious of being conscious. Consciousness is absorbed into the illusory movie world of the mind. The world of the mind is the domain of the false self. The false self is in charge of you. Then you feel disconnected from your true self, pure consciousness, and from the source of consciousness, Sri Krishna.

Awakening from the dream is accomplished by discovering your true power in the now. It is the power to choose. We all have the power of free will, which is the ability to choose where we place our attention. This is the path of intelligence. We can make a conscious choice to shift our conscious attention to the present moment. When you are present, you become conscious. When you are consciously present, you can experience the truth of who you are, which is unchanging, expansive pure awareness.

The presence of awareness does not have a beginning or end. It is changeless. When you are present, you feel connected to source. Without effort you feel satisfaction, peace and the certainty of your existence. Choosing to be present for Krishna in the sound of His Holy Name is the same thing as saying, *chant with attention, chant with love and respect.*

With folded hands, let us all stamp this advice of Bhaktivinod Thakur upon our bowed foreheads.

***"Forget the past that sleeps, and never future dream at all, but act in times that are with thee and progress thee shall call."***

# Acknowledgments

I am grateful to the following persons for their assistance in the creation of this book. Without your help and enthusiastic support, it would not have been possible for me to accomplish this task alone.

Mahaguna devi san - English to Japanese translation

Ananga Manjari san - Japanese proofreading, editing

Madhumangal san - Consultant and advisor on Japanese language and culture

Chaitanya Mangal san- Donations, Translation support

Ken San - editing, design, publications etc.

Maha laxmi dasi - Providing all details related to my books published in China, PDF files, Layouts, Photos

Lilarati Mataji- Translation from Chinese to English; coordination with publications company and designer

Bhagavat seva das- Main pillar/initiator and driving force of the project, donations, coordination with publishers, proofreading, editing etc.

Jayasri devi dasi – Follow-ups and status checks between different countries, coordination, design discussions, photos

Hari Mohan Devi Dasi - Working on recordings and transcripts for English.

Ananta Gauranga das - Tirelessly managing communications and becoming the glue holding the whole project together from start to finish.